KU-243-162

£12.99

# AN ASTONISHING SECRET

## ALSO BY DANIEL O'LEARY

BOOKS:

*Prism of Love (2000)*

*Travelling Light (2002)*

*Passion for the Possible (2003)*

*Already Within (2007)*

*Begin with the Heart (2008)*

*Unmasking God (2011)*

*Treasured and Transformed (2014)*

*The Happiness Habit (2015)*

*The Healing Habit (2016)*

*The Heavenly Habit (2017)*


AUDIO:

*Reaching for God's Light (2012)*

# AN

# ASTONISHING

# SECRET

*The Love Story of Creation*

*and the Wonder of You*

## DANIEL O'LEARY

columba press

First published in 2017 by
## columba press
23 Merrion Square North, Dublin 2
www.columba.ie

Copyright © 2017 Daniel O'Leary

All rights reserved. Without limiting the rights under copyright reserved
alone, no part of this publication may be reproduced, stored in or
introduced into a retrieval system, or transmitted, in any form or by any
means (electronic, mechanical, photocopying, recording or otherwise)
without the prior written permission of both the copyright owner and the
above publisher of the book.

ISBN: 978-1-78218-324-2

Set in Linux Libertine 10/14
Cover and book design by Alba Esteban | Columba Press
Leaves illustrations created by Freepik
Printed by ScandBook, Sweden

## THE SECRETS

*You can't grasp at the secrets*
*prise them from the earth*
*or pluck them from the air ...*
*You can't use force or even effort –*
*you can only create the right conditions*
*reverse the beam of your attention*
*and make a sacred space inside ...*
*for the secrets to flow through*
*and reveal themselves to you.*

Steve Taylor, 'The Secrets' in *The Calm Centre*


## MY BRILLIANT IMAGE

*I wish I could show you,*

*When you are lonely or in darkness,*

*The Astonishing Light*

*Of your own Being!*

Hafiz, 'My Brilliant Image, in *I Heard God Laughing,*
trans Daniel Ladinski


## MENTAL FIGHT

*You can't remake the world*

*Without remaking yourself.*

*Each new era begins within.*

Ben Okri, *Mental Fight*

# CONTENTS

# FOREWORD

Once we equate God with life itself a transformation takes place in the way we believe. Once we remove everything that separates divinity and humanity, heaven and earth, grace and nature, then we begin to truly and freely live and move in another milieu. Once we use the same name for the Gracious Mystery and Mother of all becoming, and the primal energy of creation and ongoing evolution, our faith cannot ever be the same again. And once we commit to identifying God's intimate presence in our evolving, sensual perception of the world's most beautiful artistry, creativity and imagination, in our every breath and heartbeat, in our daily darkness and invincible light, then we are living the incarnation of God in Jesus. And we are then, also, adoring the only adorable reality – the mystery of being itself. It signals the death of a God 'out there', and the birth of the God at the burning heart of Creation itself and at the core of your own being. If God could have revealed himself without the world', wrote Meister Eckhart, 'he would not have created it.' This is the revelation of an astonishing secret. It is a new moment of grace. It's like an earthquake in your heart. And you are afraid no more.

When this 'catholic, sacramental faith-imagination' becomes second nature to you, a profound simplicity envelops your soul. What is this sacramental vision? When you learn to really look at what's before you, the delight and pain that's around you; when you feel something of the hidden joy and despair of others, their desire for life and their cold despair; it is then, also, and only then, that you reach the place of intimacy with the divine, incarnate God. Jesus added nothing extra to the initial Creation. His Father had not forgotten anything! What was added, when the time was right, was the love and meaning in it all. What Jesus introduced and accomplished by his death and resurrection was not a legal contract of atonement with his demanding Father; it was the depth and invincibility of love. Love transforms darkness, death and sin. It is the very energy of Creation, of evolution. Jesus, 'the Human One', Love personified, brought a new understanding of our world and our lives, a different way of seeing everything through the lens of an unconditional love.

When everything we see, touch, hear and smell is perceived as the embrace of the divine arms; when the winter chill, the city noises, the brilliance of artists and the revelations of scientists provide glimpses of an incarnate God; when the New Universe Story captures our hearts with a profound and transforming wonder, when the courage and hope of oppressed people on a mutilated Earth are experienced as the empowering presence of the Holy Spirit within, then, and only then, are we living within the Incarnation. To do this faithfully we need a sacramental community of love around us. 'Let us pray – for the faith to recognise God's presence in our world. O God our Father, open our eyes to see you at work in the splendour of creation, in the beauty of human life. Touched by your hand our world is holy. Help us to cherish the gifts that surround us, to share your blessings with our brothers and sisters, and to experience the joy of life in your presence'.[1]

# INTRODUCTION

    The thought-provoking insights in this book will provide delightful new glimpses into your old faith. In these pages we explore some of the new insights and revelations now emerging and enriching that faith. People are finding renewed and deeper ways of being Christian, of being Catholic, of being human. A radical new light is being shed on that moment of love 2,000 years ago, when God was revealed at the centre of our lives and of our evolving world. You will want to share these rich reflections of the heart with your friends, but most of all, with your children.

    *An Astonishing Secret* offers 49 reflections on selected extracts from Pope Francis's creative writings, which invite an exciting unpacking and a creative exploring. Of the many urgent spiritual, ecological and theological themes they carry, this book focuses on one in particular – Creation and Incarnation: a deeper understanding of the closeness of a God who carefully fashioned us, who loves us unconditionally, who delights in us at every moment, and who is now flesh of our flesh, bone of our bone. The Pope is deeply concerned that we understand something of the true meaning of the Incarnation story; it is central to our faith and, unbelievably, we have mostly ignored that most beautiful mystery. He also knows that the more we grow to love our gracious Earth the more anxious we will be to reverence and protect our natural environment, and to bring compassion, peace, freedom and justice to all who are living here. This is a central theme in his encyclical *Laudato Si'*.

    *✐* Something amazing is happening. Something that could never have happened before now. A new mind-set and a new heart-set are emerging. There is a new opportunity for struggling believers to find their way once again; a radically different understanding of central dimensions of the Christian faith is now being offered. This is a profoundly moving way of seeing old teachings in a new and exciting light – a way that was impossible before recent theological renewal and startling scientific discoveries. A fresh picture of the beauty of our faith is daily becoming clearer as the treasures of science and Christianity move closer together. According to theologian and scientist Sister Ilia Delio, in the light of a new understanding of reality, of an evolution that was mostly unknown up to now, 'it is not a stretch to say that the whole theological enterprise must be rebuilt from the bottom up.' We are being offered a new mountain view with an entrancing panorama stretching out in front of us. It is time for a courageous ascent.

    *✐* We need time to read about these life-transforming moments in the journey of Christianity. We need help to grasp the depth and beauty and enormity of what is happening. We need to get acquainted with a new language so as to receive a new spiritual 'heart of flesh' based on the wonder of Creation and its evolutionary journey into the future. Nothing essential has changed in our beliefs; what is happening is that the astounding mystery is gradually revealing still more and undreamt-of possibilities to fill us with a longing to be part of it. The writings of Pope Francis range far and wide, covering a number of themes and topics, all providing rich sources of material for reflective reading and spiritual nourishment. New ideas, new scientific insights transform our faith, new efforts draw out the divine power of the human heart. Writer and preacher Richard Rohr OFM tells us that the deepest intuition of our poets, mystics and Holy Scripture are aligning with findings on the leading edge of science and empirical discovery. 'When inner and outer worlds converge like this, something beautiful is afoot – the reversal

of the centuries-long lovers' quarrel between science and spirituality, mind and heart'.[2]

    ⌇ Taking this step into playing our own different parts in the emerging scenario is a huge challenge for many. To be engaged with the renewed Christian story is to be swept along in a river of new life and creativity, a stream of graced imagination and openness that leads to a beckoning future. How can the attractiveness of the new universe story and the emerging theology of creation be gladly embraced and accepted? Who will introduce, popularise, translate and simplify some of these insights for us? But do Catholics today really *want* to know about all the amazing changes that are taking place in the renewed understanding of what the faith actually means? Is there any real desire now to light the flame again, to search for fruitful ways of a healing faith, to explore the current revelations regarding Creation and Incarnation that are bringing delight to millions? 'Indeed,' writes author Tom Inglis, 'it would seem that there is little attempt by most Irish Catholics to stimulate and invigorate their religious beliefs and practices ... The laity were, for so long, spoon-fed their beliefs and values by the church, that there is little desire or appetite to seek out new ways ...'. [3]

    ⌇ People are profoundly confused. They are caught between faith and life in an old church which is slowly splintering, and in an emerging church which is very exciting and challenging; between the old story of Creation and Fall, and the new scientific story of the universe. Geologist Fr Thomas Berry wrote, 'The Old Story – the account of how the world came to be and we how fit into it – sustained us for a long time. It shaped our emotional attitudes, provided us with a purpose, energised action, consecrated suffering, integrated knowledge, and guided education. We awoke in the morning and knew where we were. We could answer the questions of our children. But now it is no longer functioning properly – and we have not yet learned the New Story.'[4] But we are about to. In May 2017, Br Guy Consolmagno

SJ, Director of the Vatican Observatory, organised a ground-breaking conference in Castel Gandolfo, near Rome. It reiterated what past popes and theologians have been impressing on all God's people, that 'the myth of science and religion being incompatible must be finally ended', and that 'there was never anything to fear for religious believers in the theory of evolution'.

   The purpose in writing this book is to follow those guidelines, to deepen this vision, to keep digging beneath the rubble of our fading faith to find these forgotten treasures of God. The current collapsing and conflict within the institution urge us to explore deeper to find these buried and beautiful revelations about the Christian Creator-God. They are all still there, waiting to be recovered, renewed and reshaped in the light of a new impetus from the Holy Spirit, an enlightened theology of creation and incarnation, the impact of the astonishingly exciting revelations of science, and the vision of Pope Francis. There is no point, he says, in hanging on to old priorities of Church life, preserving 'adulterated forms of Christianity'. Christianity must be true to its 'eternal newness' as it dialogues 'with changing historical circumstances' (LS 121).

   Even though the content of the book is made as accessible as possible, it still grapples with huge issues, questions and connections. It must do, since it deals with mystery – the mystery of God, of Creation, of Incarnation, and of the human heart. Mystery is not something beyond the mind and imagination; it is something that cannot be fully understood by us. It is mystery that we explore, that our intellects feed upon, that is constantly revealed – but we will never be able to say, 'I know it all now!' You will never 'get' mystery – as Richard Rohr OFM says, 'It will get you!' But we do need to read, to reflect, to share and to pray about what these wonderful insights are revealing about our faith. The key, for the Christian, lies in the renewed exploration of the moment of Incarnation, and the book is really a meditation on how that moment provides, in a most attractive and enriching way, the unconditional love and meaning at the core of our faith lives. It reveals the vibrant spirituality and theology that arise when we combine the living heart of the evolving universe with the incarnate love-energy of the Creator-God.

✐   The papal writings chosen for the book will set readers' own hearts on fire, and then they will want to communicate them in their own words, and in whatever ways they can, for example in their local groups (reading/discussion/meditation), in their constant family life experiences (of growing up, faith-conversations, nature talks and walks, bedtime stories, RE homework) and in their many and varied parish pastoral ministries. Because the book is about Pope Francis's most attractive and compelling understanding of why God created us and lives in the heart of everyone, it opens many welcome windows of wonder and light at a time of too much darkness around us. Without this primary inner transformation on the part of parents, teachers, pastoral ministers and priests, the new catechisms, syllabi, curricula, liturgies and devotional practices will lack the alluring fire of the Spirit. They will not enrich and excite our hearts. (Pope Francis uses words such as 'enchant', 'fascinate' and 'seduce'.) But people will not learn it from you; they will *catch it off you.* Only transformed people transform others. From now on, children will, hopefully, carry only bright new images, words and experiences of an utterly loving Parent and Friend, pleading with us for help to restore a beautiful but broken world.

✐   But in truth, the new journey has scarcely begun. There are so many obstacles to this imaginative process of creative reconciliation. There is a selfish, maybe fearful strain within our evolving world and universe that will not surrender to the generosity of the divine spirit. Every time we hate, compete, attack, judge, disconnect, separate or block the flow of letting go, we are resisting the power of that divine love-energy that is driving and drawing Creation forward. This deadly negativity has often been most visible, and, unfortunately still is, in the relentless fear and control at the highest hierarchical levels. There is now, therefore, an extremely urgent need, at this tipping-point time for the welfare of the world and of the Church, for a wholehearted commitment to rediscovering, exploring, understanding and spreading this evergreen good news.

    ✍    In 1988, in a letter to the Director of the Vatican Observatory, Pope St John Paul II, on the occasion of a theological conference in Rome about faith and science, asked the following question: 'Does an evolutionary perspective bring any light to bear upon theology, the meaning of the human person as the *Imago Dei*, and upon the development of doctrine itself?'[5]

    ✍    Pope Francis's *Laudato Si'* provides many signposts towards a response. At an International Workshop in Rome in May 2017 for scientists and other pioneering scholars he said, 'I am deeply appreciative of your work, and I encourage you to persevere in your search for truth. For we ought never to fear truth, nor become trapped in our own preconceived ideas, but welcome new scientific discoveries with an attitude of humility.' One day soon these discoveries and theories will assume centre-stage for the thinking Church and for all who wish to stay at the living, pulsing heart of the Holy Spirit's guidance into the future. There are no options. We give it all we can. To hang back at this stage is 'to sin against God's creation'.[6] We flourish together in a new oasis of hope or we die, disillusioned, in a loveless desert.

    ✍    *An Astonishing Secret* is a small effort to appreciate, embrace and contribute to this new and fascinating renewal, especially for the sake of our children. The selected papal extracts inspire a renewed depth and intimacy in our old faith story – in the real presence of divine love folded into every twist and turn of our own unique lives and our own unique planet. They are beautiful reflections, deeply soul-stirring and utterly life-changing. In image, story and poetry they paint God in many colours – the colours of true humanity, of earth, sky and sea, of every tiny and cosmic moment of all creation.

The mystics knew this. Mechtild of Magdeburg wrote:

> The day of my spiritual awakening
> was the day I saw, and knew I saw,
> all things in God and God in all things.[7]

✍ Two themes are interwoven through the pages of this book – the mystery of Creation and the mystery of Incarnation. For the Christian these are central – the source and wellspring of all else. They are not two separate, disparate acts of God, two unconnected epic moments for the world. Rather, as Karl Rahner wrote, 'Creation and Incarnation are two moments and two phases of the *one* process of God's self-giving and self-expression ... '.[8]

✍ In this respect, writes Franciscan sister Ilia Delio, 'the whole Creation, beginning with the Big Bang, is Incarnation. Evolution is the process of unfolding life, from matter to spirit ... The God of evolution is the God of adventure, a God who loves to do new things and is always new. We are invited into this adventure of love to find our freedom in love, and to love without measure'.[9] Every line in this book aims to create a deeper intimacy between you, the world and the beautiful artist and lover we still call God – God-made-Creation, God-made-flesh, God-made-bread, God-made-everything.

✍ Faith continually needs to be stripped of its social, historical and systemic encrustations, and returned to its first churchless incarnation in the human heart. 'The world itself,' writes Mark Patrick Hederman in the *The Furrow*, 'is the universal religion that precedes all organised religions. Nature is the first scripture where we read the word of God' (April 2017). In Romans 1: 20 we find, 'Ever since the creation of the world, God's power and divinity – however invisible – have become visible for the mind to see in all the things that God has made'. 'There is no need for temples,' preached the 14th Dalai Lama, 'no need for complicated philosophy. Our own brain, our own heart is our temple.' 'The Kingdom is within your own hearts', said Jesus (Lk 17: 21). Your core, your DNA are already and always divine. It is the Spirit of Love implanted in you by your Creator-Mother at the first moment of your being. The only real reason for religion is to protect and nourish the blossoming, in community, of that first seed of love for all creation.

 ⌇ 'A Further Word' at the end of each reflection offers insights into the depths of the fundamental love story at the heart of this book. In accessible language, and in the context of 'the bigger picture', it invites readers to further deepen their understanding of the main reflection themes in the light of safe theological scholarship and accepted scientific research. Christian commentators predict that this 'bigger picture' is of immense significance, and that it will, and it must, dominate our courageous conversations around Christianity and science from now on – God's gradual self-revelation in two stories, the unfolding story of an evolving Earth and the definitive story called Incarnation. Our Christian churches are already lagging alarmingly behind in taking these remarkable mysteries seriously. 'Participation in evolution is not an option for the baptised faithful', Ilia Delio reminds us in *The Emergent Christ*. 'It is essential to the core of our faith in Jesus Christ.'[10] Not to get involved, Pope Francis warns us, is a 'sin'.

 ⌇ There are countless windows of wonder into the heart of the Incarnation mystery. 'A Further Word' expands our understanding of the central 'love story' themes so as to further deepen our grasp of the beautiful mystery. They help us prepare ourselves for the startling revelation that emerges when we weave together the threads of the amazing process called The New Universe Story of evolving Creation into the pattern of the evolving Story of Incarnation. It is not the easiest step to take. But it is already beginning to influence our theology, spirituality, pastoral ministry and our personal relationship with God and each other more than we may imagine at the moment. Soon it will be mainstream teaching. It has to be. (In a very real sense, this bigger, wider and deeper story of Creation has always been at the centre of Christian teaching. I have tried to indicate this throughout the book. But in the light of current theological and scientific progress, it is beginning to impact our world in a most significant way.)

    ✐   We are now in between those two powerful stories – Creation and Incarnation. In *The Dream of the Earth* Thomas Berry writes of the story that religion tells and the story that science tells. For many of us the stories have clashed as we felt that one was right and the other was wrong. But a new moment is emerging – the moment that brings the two stories into a meeting place where they complement each other, shaping yet more clearly a new outline of what is true, shedding a welcome light on both the gifts of religion and the gifts of scientific exploration. 'Science without religion is lame,' wrote Albert Einstein, 'and religion without science is blind'. We now know that we are living in a very unfinished universe still at the dawn of its creation, a universe that is still evolving and will continue forever to do so. This insight is central to the reflections in this book. In taking these remarkable realities seriously Christianity, and particularly the Catholic Church, are already lagging behind alarmingly (according to Cardinal Carlo Maria Martini, by 200 years). 'Participation in evolution is not an option for the baptised faithful; it is essential to the core of our faith in Jesus Christ.'[11]

    ✐   So many Catholic Christians are disillusioned with an institution that is reluctant to, or incapable of re-visioning and restructuring itself, of developing its theology, of reframing its beliefs within the relentless challenges of an emerging world-consciousness. 'It is imperative', writes Kevin Treston, 'that Christianity reformulate its beliefs and liturgical practices which resonate with the world of revolutionary science, globalisation, internet, sociology, and social sciences.'[12] Millions of Catholics wish to stay connected to their Church but find it increasingly difficult to do so because of its continuing resistance to the current revelations of the New Universe Story. So much is happening in the world of science as it daily sheds a wonderful light on the nature of Creation and its evolution. And if we get that wrong, as St Thomas Aquinas reminded us many centuries ago, 'we get God wrong'. It is evolutionary connection rather than doctrinal correction that will convince a new and younger generation by opening up for them fascinating new approaches to the love and meaning at the heart of Creation, at the heart of evolution, at the heart of Incarnation, at the heart of God.

✐     In *From Teilhard to Omega* Delio writes, 'Christians who profess to love God and have been saved by Christ, I believe, will lose nothing and gain everything by transplanting (expanding) their devotion to the new incalculably larger setting offered by contemporary biology and cosmology. Our sense of the Creator, the work of the Holy Spirit, and the redemptive significance of Christ can now grow by immense orders of magnitude. The Love that rules the stars will now have to be seen as embracing two hundred billion galaxies, a cosmic epic of fourteen billion years' duration, and perhaps even a multiverse. Our thoughts about Christ and redemption will have to extend over the full breadth of cosmic time and space.'[13]

✐     Not many of us are theologians or scientists; fewer still are both. But, as we have already observed, our saints and scholars encourage us, to the best of our abilities, to be forever seeking the reasons for our faith – *fides quaerens intellectum* (St Anselm). That is why, in each 'A Further Word' there is a reliance on the thoughts and faith-imagination of wiser people – trusted scholars and scientific experts within the believing community who are beginning to suggest an outline, a direction, a horizon for the exciting times ahead when both disciplines come closer together, painstakingly completing each other, shedding an ever-widening and ever-deepening light on the most alluring mystery of an evolving universe energised by the love of God. There are gifted writers, some of them quoted here, now embarking on the task of taking up this challenge, and there are millions of Catholic Christians ready to receive, question and rejoice in these panoramic presentations of the Christian faith. (To provide the best and most inspiring sources I rely especially on the works of Pierre Teilhard de Chardin and Ilia Delio, both accepted as safe guides into the adventure of belonging to an emerging Church.) This book is an attempt to prepare the soil of our hearts for an exciting new sowing.

✐　Today, an educated Catholic laity, familiar with intellectual rigour and well read in matters scientific, believes that the concept of Creation and its evolution is at a vital and timely place for an urgent review of many of our teachings. 'Modern science and technology offer a new threshold of consciousness for Christianity to enter and reframe its core narrative.' writes Kevin Treston. 'The profound sacred myths in the Christ story stimulate imaginative responses to the new questions of life ... The Incarnation is ongoing, both as the advent of Jesus in history, and the cosmic Incarnation of God within the expanding universe. Dialogue, scholarship, discourse, listening to the heartbeats of the world and creation itself will ground the Good News in the everyday lives of people.'[14]

✐　'A Further Word' is not about getting into scholarly scientific or theological details concerning the epic crossroads at which we now find ourselves. Many excellent attempts to do this are currently available. The purpose, rather, is to emphasise for struggling, searching and still faithful believers, no matter how confused they may be initially, the fact that we are on the threshold of an immense moment in an emerging love story; and to introduce the need for all of us to play a part in decisions and actions that will re-energise the Catholic Christian Church. A liberating, inviting cosmic energy is now beginning to release some astonishing truths that are streaming from the heart of Incarnation. Pope Francis urges us to take the time and trouble to become more aware of, more interested in and more excited by the undreamt-of horizons opening up before us. It now seems as though it is not possible to talk, teach, preach or write about God or Christianity except against the astonishing background of an evolving Creation. This is a challenge that will not go away.

    ✐   Who will teach us to revisit, re-vision, reinterpret, re-understand our familiar beliefs, teachings, practices and spiritualities in an evolutionary context? Who will tell us how to 'do theology' against this new background, to study the Gospels, to celebrate the Eucharist, to teach, to preach, to live our lives so as to embrace this paradigm shift in our perspectives of the world and of our faith? Who will reassure us that the pursuit of justice, peace, freedom and equality will be enhanced, that ecumenical efforts within and between world religions will all be fundamentally strengthened by a shared belief in this startling breakthrough into a perspective that is bigger than any one religion, that echoes the 'magnanimity' to which Pope Francis has committed his life? Throughout his spiritual writings theologian Ronald Rolheiser OMI reminds us that God is the author of creation, of all that is good and true. For that reason, he holds, no one religion or culture contains all of the truth. We must be open to perceive and receive goodness from many different sources. Pope Francis challenges us to expand our thinking by allowing a new wisdom to shape the understanding of our faith, our world and our images of God. The way we ponder on the wonder of our Gracious Creator, on Creation, salvation, suffering and death, now needs to be done in a wider context because life itself is unfolding against an ever-widening horizon. This will bring new tensions and enriching paradoxes into the way we live our lives in faith.

    ✐   As with any visionary glimpse of a new horizon, perseverance, attention and application are essential. You will need a dogged faith. But the veils will part. See it as a fresh start. We need to approach our old faith with what Zen practitioners call a 'Beginner's Mind'. We need to drop much unnecessary and unhelpful baggage from the past, and employ our holy imaginations for the future. This is a new and exciting beginning where the faith takes on a totally undreamt-of challenge and transformation. It is like a new window on a new world springing from a radically renewed faith. It is far too soon to put a full stop to the story of our universe and of our God – a story that, in fact, has scarcely begun.

🖉   The contents of 'A Further Word' have been chosen to build on the contents of the reflections they follow by pointing to wider, deeper and ultimately inevitable horizons that await all those who are adventurous enough to believe in a beckoning future, and to bravely set foot on one of the uncharted paths that will bring us safely home. With their insightful extracts, they are offered for your imagination, your curiosity, your faithful seeking for the truth. They will stretch your mind and imagination. Some are poetic, some are mystical, some are scientific, but they are all the sincere considerations of visionary women and men. (The word 'mystic' is used throughout this book. It is not a reference to any privileged, esoteric or rare attribute of special people. There is a mystical dimension to every human heart. It emphasises experiential awareness over cerebral knowledge, beyond textbook information; it is the capacity of every human being for wonder and mystery.)

🖉   Try to see the 49 extracts or passages, each followed by a reflection and 'A Further Word', as a collection of spotlights shining from different angles on an emerging threshold. If one extract baffles you, then try another. They can all stand on their own. Feel free to dip into them. They are but hints, hunches, stepping stones to a place of immense meaning and mystery. Try to connect the ideas as best you can. Some issues are deliberately repeated. They offer various vantage points to help you form a general outline of a new horizon as, building on the best of our tradition and on current understanding of things, science and religion draw ever closer together. And then our wisdom, our vision, our love and adoration of a creative Mother-God will transform the quality of our faith, of our human lives, of our new awareness and experience of love. There will be a new freedom in our ever-alluring ways of telling the love story. Our children deserve no less.

...........................................................................................................

Note: All 49 extracts discussed in this book are taken from *Laudato Si' (LS)* and *Evangelii Gaudium (EG)*.

# THE
# REFLECTIONS

# 1

## LOVING THE EARTH – GOD'S LIVING BODY

*St Francis reminds us that our common home is like a sis-*
*ter with whom we share our life and a beautiful mother who*
*opens her arms to embrace us.* [LS 1]

This is a long way from the fearsome teaching of the past regarding
'the world, the flesh and the devil', a negative story that frightened us
when we were children, a story about the fall-out from the Adam and
Eve myth that many Catholics still believe. Pope Francis knows that the
world is good, as God pronounces it in Genesis; it is not a punishment
for an 'original sin' that never happened! (to be discussed more fully
later). Even at this time of serious darkness for Christian churches there
are stirrings of a new light from deep within. Because we are born with
God's own longing safely incarnate within us, we will forever seek that
harmony and hope for which we were born. As the river flows and
the bird flies, the human heart will always long for completion in love.
Pope Francis knows this. It is why he acts, speaks and writes as he does.
It is, for instance, why he sees creation as 'a beautiful mother'.

He knows that something invariably stirs in us when we stop to
look around us with eyes of wonder, with what he often calls 'the
contemplative gaze'. We begin to see more deeply into the beauty of
'ordinary' things – the speeding train through the sleeping fields, the
flash of a wing from a hidden nest, the whistle of the wind through
November trees, the way a cat looks at you. We see daily happenings and events – mornings, tears, hills, water, seasons, births, bodies,
babies, death, growing – with a new light around them, a forgotten
vision now being recovered, some kind of promise of heaven restored.
How utterly liberating it is for us to have a leader who encourages
us to see this wonderful world as we would a lover, full of grace
and blessing! Somewhere in our hearts we have always known and

delighted in this vision in a natural, instinctual kind of way. And now we know, that hunch, that stirring, that lifting of the human spirit is another name for God's presence, for the deepest reason for our reaching, for the joy we never tire of seeking. The heaven we live for is not a place waiting in the future; it lies at our feet, at our fingertips, in what our eyes see and our tongue tastes.

At last we are learning how to love the land we live on, how to walk beautifully on the fields and streets around us. This is a much more evolutionary step for humanity than walking on the moon. Our Celtic forebears did not disrespect their environment; they saw it as a precious aspect of their lives. So did the native peoples of many lands. Too often, a mistaken religious emphasis has sundered the close bonds between God's love and Creation itself. Our world is not just a useful resource, a place to live on, to supply us with food, to be exploited for our benefit, 'to be plundered at will' – and then to be left behind as we head for heaven. She is a living, breathing, precious entity to be cherished daily.

Only when we begin behaving as though the Earth is our true home does it begin to really feel like one. We may each have a different religion, language, culture or skin colour, but under the one sky we all belong to one human race, one planet in one universe of immense beauty. And, as Pope Francis has taught, all are *equally* the people of God. Until we expand the horizons of our hearts and minds we will never feel the consolation of being at home, but of feeling lost and cautious on a foreign shore. There are levels of living that we have still not experienced. There are depths of belonging to our environment that are as yet unknown to us. Yet it was to experience this depth that we were born. Until we see the world we live in, beautiful and broken though it may be, with a tender care, and love it as we would our own family, we will never experience the abundant life promised to all God's beloved creatures – that is everyone and everything. And every morning we are born again to that possibility.

It will take time, for many of us, really to grasp the intimacy between God and the world, between grace and nature, between the holy and the human. Divine love is at the core of creation, from the panorama of oceans and milky ways, to the length of an ant's leg. And that love is urging everything to risk, to move forward, to trust. 'Beside every blade of grass,' the Talmud tells us, 'there is an angel that bends over and whispers "Grow, Grow".' We know all about this because of the unexplored mystery of the Incarnation, the very core and hinge of our faith. The presence of the incarnate Word fills everything with God's very being. It graces nature, it consecrates time, it divinises humanity, it blesses every effort for good. As Pope Francis keeps reminding us, through Christ, God is present in the entire cosmos, from the tiniest particle of matter to the infinity of space. The whole world is incarnational. 'Through him, with him, in him' everything, every person, all that happens, is created, sustained and sanctified.

## A FURTHER WORD

*To understand Pope Francis's opening sentence more clearly we need to expand our understanding and viewpoints, to see them against a wider, cosmic horizon. We then revise, recalculate and reshape our opinions, theories and theologies. And then we begin to love as never before. In spatial terms, to give us a clearer perspective, to deepen our sense of wonder, how big is 'the bigger picture'?*

'Today the Christian is aware of living on a tiny planet that is part of a system of a particular sun which itself belongs to a galaxy with 300 million stars and is hundreds and thousands of light-years broad, a galaxy estimated to be but one among billions in the universe. It is not easy for an individual to see Earth as the reality for which the universe exists. In this cosmos of gigantic dimensions, a size not even able to be imagined, human beings can feel themselves to be little more than an accidental marginal phenomenon ... the eternal Logos of God who drives forward these billions of galaxies has become a human being on this small planet which is but a speck of dust in the universe.'[15] Since Karl Rahner wrote this, the cosmic estimations he offers have expanded even more astonishingly. He is referring here to the many new challenges that face the Christian story on planet Earth in light of the seemingly infinite cosmic milieu in which we find ourselves.

In *Vast Universe* Professor Thomas O'Meara OP says, 'If there are billions of galaxies, each with billions of stars, the chances are that hundreds of thousands of planets have civilisations. They are not all existing now: some have come and gone, fading away into God's providence hundreds of millions of years ago. Others will begin to exist far into the future. Still, thousands of civilisations might live in our own space and time.'[16]

# 2

## WE ARE BLIND – TO THE SICKNESS OF OUR MOTHER-EARTH

*The violence present in our hearts, wounded by sin, is also reflected in the symptoms of sickness evident in the soil, in the water, in the air and in all forms of life ... We have forgotten that we ourselves are dust of the earth (Gen 2: 7); our very bodies are made up of her elements; we breathe her air and we receive life and refreshment from her waters. [LS 2]*

Pope Francis laments, 'The violence in our hearts, wounded by sin ... against our Mother Earth by our irresponsible use and abuse of the goods which God has endowed her'. Lord Deben, Chair of the UK's Independent Committee on Climate Change writes, 'We are diminishing, damaging and ultimately destroying ourselves.' It is here that the encyclical *Laudato Si'* is so telling. It reminds us of our sinful assertion that we are the masters now, embracing the values of a throwaway society. 'This attitude,' the Pope warns us, 'then extends to fragile humanity itself. The old, the disabled, the unborn are too often seen as inconvenient, and their intrinsic worth is ignored.' (*LS* 43) The 'poor' are always the first victims of human abuse of the earth. This terrible destruction stems from our loss of intimacy with, our loss of care or concern for our Mother Earth. An inhuman, reckless greed has wreaked havoc on innocent creatures, human and non-human.

The Pope reminds us that we are created from the Earth, our bodies sustained by nature's elements, our very lives kept in being by breathing her air, our energies and health preserved by her healing water. There is a Celtic awareness of the remedies for human ailment in nature itself – potassium, magnesium, selenium, iron, zinc, calcium, vitamin D and various other minerals and vitamins. A sacred healing fills the natural environment we live in (above). There is a mutual dependence that we too often, at our peril, ignore. *Laudato Si'* is an urgent wake-up call. Are we protecting the Earth as we would our mother, our sister? Are we deeply concerned about its future? Do we fully appreciate, even believe, the Pope asks, her role of living praise? He keeps emphasising the worship offered by the universe to God, a theme beloved of St Francis himself.

> There is no bird on the wind,
> There is no star in the sky,
> There is nothing beneath the sun
> But proclaims his goodness.[17]

And do we know that we humans have evolved, in a precious moment of creation, into the locus and focus of the Earth's consciousness and awareness? Without us she is blind and vulnerable, unfinished and 'groaning' (St Paul). We can tell the Earth that she is our nourishment and inspiration – holding us, mothering us. 'The new awareness that is sweeping our planet reminds us that we are so interconnected with the air we breathe, the trees of the forest, the flowers of the field, the mountains and rivers, that their diminishment is our diminishment, their destruction our destruction. Not only the beauty and majesty but also the chaos and power of the natural world inspire our poetry, our art, and our spiritual lives with a sense of wonder. When we fan this flame of wonder in our heart there is a new meaning in our lives.'[18]

Pope Francis is practical – and in a hurry. He knows that until we believe the Earth to be a precious, long-suffering family member, the damaged body of God, we will persevere in our carelessness towards it. He is well aware of the unfortunate consequences of a deeply flawed teaching about God's banishment of all of us as exiles to 'this vale of tears' where death happens. And in this particular passage he issues a warning. The Earth and ourselves are inseparably and intrinsically connected. The pain of one is the pain of the other. In his *Message for the World Day of Peace*, 2014, he said, 'Nature is at

our disposition and we are called to exercise a responsible steward-
ship over it. Yet so often we are driven by greed and by the arrogance
of dominion, possession, manipulation and exploitation; we do not
preserve nature; nor do we respect it or consider it as a gracious gift
which we must care for and set at the service of our brothers and sisters, including future generations.'

In the meantime a first step may well be to soften our own hearts
to the tender power of nature, to experience in our deepest selves
that profound bonding and intimacy that can flood our senses when
we surrender to the incarnate beauty of God. It is this kind of unforgettable experience that transforms our attitudes, values and goals.
There is a neglected mystic in all of us, waiting to be nourished by this
beauty. 'I walked out alone in the evening,' wrote Bede Griffiths OSB.
'A lark rose suddenly from the ground beside the tree by which I was
standing, and poured out its song above my head, and then sank –
still singing – to rest ... I felt inclined to kneel to the ground as though
I had been standing in the presence of an angel ...'.[19]

## A FURTHER WORD

*'Why', the Pope asks, 'have we forgotten that we are of the
earth ... ?' And why are we so resistant to the openness he
is pleading for? Many of us know we must knuckle down
to some serious reading, have lively conversations with our
friends, indulge in imaginative thinking and ask a hundred
questions. One question that quickly appears is the one
about 'original sin'. How does it 'fit in' with the Universe
Story of original love and joy?*

'The new emerging Christian consciousness, or, I might say, the new
emerging *catholic* consciousness, cannot and must not be suppressed.
Information technology is enhancing the speed of its evolution, and
it is taking root at the most basic level of individual lives. As with
evolutionary emergence on the whole, the new emerging catholic

consciousness is encountering resistance to change on various levels: the institutional church, academic theology and ecclesial life ... On every level, whether it is resistance to the new theology or the refusal of pluralism, the inability to let go of medieval theology and engage the world as science informs us. Hence, there is resistance to relate to God in a new way, in a new world, to see the God of Jesus Christ as the God who does new things, the God of hope and promise ... It is difficult to say for certain, but is seems the church is slowly collapsing from within. Instead of evolving it is devolving – its very presence is thinning out to the extent that in some areas of the world, such as parts of Western Europe, it is dissolving into history ... [But] death is part of new life. Are we experiencing a necessary death today in the Body of Christ, the Church? Is the Church experiencing a weakness of heart from within because there is no longer sufficient spirit of life to sustain itself? Are we on the brink of resurrection or revolution?'[20]

Theologians suggest, especially today, that what is meant by 'original sin' is the given human condition into which each of us is born, a potential to damage humanity, to diminish altruism and destroy love – a condition we all share and by which we are all affected. The 'sin of the world', in which we are all connected, is the biblical term for it. It is more about the darkness and evil that awaits the innocent child after birth and baptism, rather than about any contamination she is bringing into the world with her, and that needs to be exorcised out of her (cf. the baptismal ceremony exorcism). Sharing in the human condition does not mean that the sin of Adam and Eve, who never existed in the first place, has already shadowed the heart of the already-graced child. Karl Rahner writes, ' ... original sin in no way means that the moral quality of the actions of the first person or persons is transmitted to us, whether this be through a juridical imputation by God, or through some kind of biological heredity, however conceived.'[21]

'In other words,' writes teacher Judy Cannato, 'we are not personally accountable for the human condition. An original sin is not imputed to us and we are not required to make amends for a "fall".

Nor does original sin mean that we have been born depraved (fallen, excluded, stripped of divine love) ... An evolutionary point of view does not deny or contradict the reality of personal and collective sin. What it does reject is literal thinking that there was an Eden – a place on Earth in which human life was completely in conscious relationship with the Holy, and to which we will return if we regain right relationship with God. In this context there is no paradise to recapture.'[22]

# 3

## THE HUMAN STAIN - WE SIN AGAINST OUR OWN EARTHLY FAMILY

*Patriarch Bartholomew has spoken of our need to repent of the ways we have harmed the planet ... For humans to destroy the biological diversity of God's creation, to degrade the integrity of the earth by causing changes in the climate, to strip the earth of its natural forests or to destroy its wetlands, to contaminate the earth's waters, its land or its air and its life, to commit a crime against the natural world – these are sins against ourselves and a sin against God. [LS 8]*

Aware of Eastern Orthodoxy and its concerns about the environment, Pope Francis has worked closely with Patriarch Bartholomew and frequently quotes him on their mutual understanding of 'an environmental sin' – the crime that has been committed against the natural world by polluting it, plundering its resources and degrading its integrity by ignoring the ravages of climate change. At the root of this sin is the denial of our vocation as 'priests and priestesses of Creation' (this will be discussed later). The Pope reserves the word 'sin' for our wilful ignorance of the holiness of our planet, and for anything we do to hurt or diminish her in any way.

We are born into life, and we are baptised into Christianity to build the kingdom, to form unity and deepen belonging, to protect our community, including our Mother Earth and Sister Nature. The Pope is clarifying the fact that any refusal to do this can be called a serious 'sin against ourselves and against God'. Strong language! There can be no greater indication of the evil of this attitude. (But we were never told very much about that until now.) When we resist the inclination towards strengthening the common good, when we ignore the opportunities for playing our part in the nourishment of

God's incarnate body – our planet – when we refuse to change and grow through supporting and protecting everything created, then we are serious and serial sinners. *An Astonishing Secret* tries to offer a radically alternative emphasis – an enchanting story to enable us to fall in love again with God.

'Sin,' writes Ilia Delio, 'is the refusal to participate in the web of life. It describes the personal history of one who was created for communion – and refuses it. It is the rejection of our identity as part of an interdependent world in which God's power expresses itself through shared power with other creatures. Sin is the refusal to accept responsibility for those to whom we are connected ... It signifies the current alienation of nature from humanity, its estrangement from God and from its own creative possibilities envisaged by God from the outset of creation. Sin is the refusal to be a person of true relationship, which results in a broken human community and environment.'[23]

Today, the damage to love is the measure of sin. And the emphasis is moving beyond our personal sins to a more communal, systemic understanding of it. We can now say that anything unloving, unforgiving, anything that blocks, divides or thwarts community, whatever deliberately keeps things separate and seduces people from the one task of creating a final Communion of Love – carries the deadly edge of sin. (And most of our religious institutions are guilty of these attitudes.) Since divine love is the motivation, energy, source and destiny of Creation and its evolution, then it is God's own essence we are denying and destroying. Sin is blind to all of this. It does not notice the vulnerable beauty of nature that silently yearns for our protection. Where grace sees goodness and blessing, sin looks through cynical eyes. It lacks the imagination to comprehend and feel the vibrant presence of God, always, everywhere.

In scriptural terms sin is seen as 'missing the mark', losing the plot, getting hopelessly distracted from the original horizon of a final fulfilment in love. There is no magic or mystery in the flat world of sin. In his famous *Original Blessing* Matthew Fox wrote, 'By sinning in these ways we refuse to fall in love with life, to love what is loveable, to befriend life's simple and non-elitist pleasures, to celebrate the blessings of life, to return thanks for such blessing by still more blessing.'24 We must now rebuild on a foundation of original goodness, and not on a foundation of original sin or original curse. That rebuilding would focus our consciousness, at least in part, on the wider picture of our responsibility as Christian human beings for the welfare of our Mother Earth. Pope Francis sees this as the call to 'ecological conversion'. This conversion emerges from a more enlightened awareness. As Hugh O'Donnell tells us, 'Mindless pollution, careless attitudes towards the rights of other species, the creation of excessive waste through excessive consumption, call for new eyes and ears. For when we sin against the earth, we sin against ourselves and sin against succeeding generations of children.'25

Zachary Hayes OFM develops this further. 'Sin is not a mere infringement of a law extrinsic to our nature. It is a failure to realise the potential of our nature. If our nature is fundamentally a potential to expand, sin is a relentless contradiction of that potential. If the history of evolution up to the emergence of humanity appears a relatively consistent line of increased consciousness, with sin a reverse force has entered history. Sin is a resistance to expansion through union with others ... Sin is a failure in the collaborative effort to move toward full personalisation in human community. If sin is the history of the negative response to God leading to alienation, separation and isolation, the positive response is the history of grace leading to ever deeper union among human beings and of humanity with God.'26

## A FURTHER WORD

*Pope Francis writes passionately of the human 'crime', the 'sin', the 'destruction of creation'. If the arrival of Jesus was not primarily about rescuing a sinful, guilty and banished human race from the continuing exile of our lives by a terrible death on a cross, what, in light of the evolutionary process, do we believe about the Saviour now?*

'To talk about Jesus,' writes Delio, 'as the person of radically new consciousness within history puts a new emphasis on the purpose of the incarnation. Since the eleventh century Western Christology has held fast to sin as the primary reason for Christ. Anselm of Canterbury said that the incarnation was necessary to repay the debt due because of the sin of Adam and Eve. Although Western Christology has focused on an original sin as the reason for Christ, there is no reference to Adam and Eve anywhere else in the Bible (nor does Jesus ever refer to them!) which has led scholars to conclude that the story was added relatively late in Israel's history in response to creation myths of its ancient Near Eastern neighbours ... Seeing the incarnation as the (definitive) emergence of God in the history of the universe, that is, as the inner pressure of love at the heart of the universe, gives new meaning to evolution and to sin as part of an evolutionary world.'[27] Jesus died to reveal to the universe the depth, the limitlessness, the cost of human/divine love that is the beginning and the end of everything. He died so we would never again fear death.

'To explore the meaning of Jesus Christ in evolution, it is helpful to keep several ideas in mind. The first is that creation and incarnation are not two separate events but one process of God's self-giving and self-communication. When we talk about incarnation we are also talking about creation. The God who creates is the God who saves because salvation *is* new creation. Second, whatever we say about creation, we are saying about God. Creation expresses the Creator; it is an outward expression of God's love and grace. Creation is the book that tells us about God, because God is the author of creation. Third, God is dynamic, trinitarian love, which means that love is the source, meaning and goal of creation. Love is not added onto creation, like an outer coat of paint that makes creation nice and pretty; rather, love defines created reality.'[28]

Jesus Christ did not come for just a 33-year visit to our planet so that he could die for our sins and then go back to heaven. He was here from the beginning. 'Christ is present in the entire cosmos, from the least particle of matter to the convergent human community. The whole cosmos is incarnational. Christ is the instrument, the centre, the end of the whole of animate and material creation; through him, everything is created, sanctified and vivified ... Every act of evolving nature is the self-expression of God, since the very act of nature's growth is the energy of divine love. God unfolds in the details of nature; thus, evolution is not only *of* God but *is* God incarnate ... In Jesus something new emerges, a new consciousness, a new related-ness, and a new immediacy to God's presence – in short, another 'Flaring Forth' like the Big Bang. Jesus symbolises a new unity in creation – non-duality, reconciling love, healing mercy and compassion. Jesus brings a new heart to humanity, both on the individual and collective planes.'[29]

# 4

## THE WORLD, GOD'S HOME, IS THE FIRST SACRAMENT

*As Christians we are called to accept the world as a sacrament of communion, as a way of sharing with God and our neighbours on a global scale. It is our humble conviction that the divine and the human meet in the slightest detail in the seamless garment of God's creation, in the least speck of dust of our planet. [LS 9]*

These papal words are so exciting. Do you believe them? Does the Institutional Church believe them? They fling wide the doors of our imagination. They reveal the beautiful, interlocked, beating hearts of Creation and Incarnation. They banish the darkness of the flawed doctrines around Adam and Eve and their 'original sin', and introduce the hidden story of a Mother God who created us out of love, and who forever loves us to bits, no matter what. This world is the divine body of God in space and time. So are we all. At birth we are born as pure and shining as we will ever be, as innocent and as close to God as any saint. There is no original sin that needs to be washed away from the baby's soul.

It was when God became human flesh in Jesus that all these delightful truths were fully revealed to us. For some strange reason most of us were never told about them. At that unique moment our lives were radically changed for ever. We became aware that we are now called to recognise God in everything that happens, in the circumstances of our daily existence, in all that exists. God is revealed in the midst, the mess and the mystery all around us. The Pope's astonishing 'humble conviction' means there is a huge shift and surge in our perception of creation, in our way of looking at things, in our own inner self-awareness. It profoundly colours the quality of our lives; it influences the manner in which we face each day, each trouble, each new encounter. It infuses a true, graced meaning into our pain; it doubles our joys; it transforms our lives. For all of this gradually to find its home in our hearts, we need to use the creativity and imagination inspired within us by the Holy Spirit. Our Pope often refers to these blessed gifts of each human heart.

This spirituality is about sensing the gold in the vicissitudes of life, about divining 'the dearest freshness deep down things',[30] about touching God in the utter ordinariness of each day, bringing a new sense of depth to all our experiences. The Pope's most life-changing and faith-changing words, about the fact that God is revealed and experienced within the vital world of our senses and our daily lives, in everything that happens to us, and at the core of creation itself, seems like a whole new context and ground-plan for Christian belief, a kind of revolution that changes everything. All our lives and stories are God's lives and stories too.

Given the relentless and damaging indoctrination of the past, this recovered love story will take time to seep into young souls, to awaken our hearts, to excite our minds. But this love story does not deny that crucially, we must never forget that, despite being made in God's image, we are all tainted with 'the human stain', what scripture calls 'the sin of the world', a condition that we cannot explain. Something in our deepest soul reaches for the darkness, for the loveless way, even for evil in its many disguises. Why are we so prone to knock down as well as to build up, to destroy as well as to restore, to be afraid rather than to choose courage? From where does that destructive energy and obsession come? Creation was to have been perfected and transfigured by human beings, lifting it up and revealing its potential for participation in the life of the Creator God. 'But humanity,' the Pope reflects, 'refused to see Creation as an icon of the Word of God through whom it was made and holds together' (Col 1:16–17). Humans, greedy and reckless, denied that Creation was an ever-present sacrament of thanksgiving by which they might be in constant communion with God.

Christ, however, has achieved what humanity alone could not. By his birth, death and resurrection he reveals the inseparable communion and intimacy between God and creation in every tiny mote invisible to the eye, 'in the least speck of dust'. Christ, who in assuming human nature united himself with Creation, comes to save not only humanity but also the whole cosmos (Col 1: 20). *Laudato Si'* emphasises that humanity needs a huge change of mind, a *metanoia,* a paradigm shift, so as to believe in our own uniqueness, in our wider responsibility, and to live in humble and glad harmony with Creation. Can we take at least some of this truth into our hearts – because, in God's design, we were created to hear it?

And how do we share, teach, tell, preach about these breathtaking revelations to children, to all who were born to hear such life-giving news? It is important to remember that we are all created out of divine love, and because of that, the ears of our heart are always open to hear and welcome the amazing good news we are trying to understand in these pages. The difficulties we experience are mostly due to the damaged preaching and teaching of our childhood and later years – even now – and also to that sinister resistance (the sin of the world, the human stain) that we all carry to a wholehearted acceptance and delight in the news of a very human God.

## A FURTHER WORD

*Are we saying that all Creation from the very beginning, all matter, nature itself are to be seen as truly spiritual, God's own incarnate essence? Is this is the vital question that lies at the heart of our understanding of Incarnation?*

Elizabeth Johnson tells us that 'Seen in the light [of Incarnation] the natural world, instead of being divorced from what is sacred, takes on a sacramental character. Sacramental theology has always taught that simple material things – water, oil, bread and wine – can be bearers of divine grace. This is so, it now becomes clear, only because to begin with, the whole physical world itself is the matrix of God's gracious indwelling. Matter bears the mark of the sacred and has itself a spiritual radiance. In turn, divine presence is sacramentally mediated in and through the world's embodiment, not necessarily nor absolutely, but graciously and really. The indwelling Spirit of God moves over the void, breathes into the chaos, quickens, warms, sets free, blesses and continuously creates the world, empowering its evolutionary advance. Bringing the Spirit back into the picture this way, leads ecological theology to envision God, not at, or beyond, the apex of the pyramid of being, as in modern theism, but within and around the emerging, struggling, living, dying and renewing circle of life and the whole universe itself.'[31]

The Pope's phrase 'sacramental world' is a key concept in his understanding of Creation and Incarnation. It means that God comes to us in the guise of all aspects of Creation; that God is experienced in all our human experiences. We need to meditate on this astonishing revelation.

'Scripture tells us,' writes Ilia Delio, 'that God is Creator, revealed in Jesus Christ, and the Christian tradition says that the Creator is expressed in creation. Creation is a "book"; it is God's self-expression. As God expresses the God-self in creation, creation in turn expresses the Creator. Every aspect of creation is an aspect of God's self-expression because every creature has its foundation in the Word and is equally close to God. The world is sacramental because the divine Word of God is expressed in the manifold variety of creation; it is a symbolic world and full of signs of God's presence ... From the Big Bang to the present moment the universe is God-filled, divine-love-engendered matter; the evolution of the universe is the coming to be of Christ. Evolution is not opposed to religion; it does not contradict the God of Jesus Christ. Rather it opens up a new window to the divine mystery.'[32]

Pierre Teilhard de Chardin reassures that '... [Thus] science should not disturb our faith by its analyses. Rather, it should help us to know God better, to understand and appreciate him more fully. Personally,

I am convinced that there is no more substantial nourishment for the spiritual life than contact with scientific realities, if they are properly understood. The person who habitually lives in the society of the elements of this world, who personally experiences the overwhelming immensity of things and their wretched dissociation, that person, I am certain, becomes more acutely conscious than anyone of the tremendous need for the unity that continually drives the universe further ahead, and of the fantastic future ahead, and of the fantastic future that awaits it.

'... No one understands so fully as the person who is absorbed in the study of matter to what a degree Christ, through his incarnation, is interior to the world, rooted in the world even in the heart of the tiniest atom ... It is useless, in consequence, and it is unfair, to oppose science and Christ, or to separate them as two domains alien to one another. By itself, science cannot discover Christ, but Christ satisfies the yearnings that are born in our hearts in the school of science.'[33]

# 5

## THE HOLINESS OF FALLING IN LOVE

*St Francis invites us to see nature as a magnificent book in which God speaks to us and grants to us a glimpse of his infinite beauty and goodness. Beyond the language of mathematics and biology he takes us to the heart of what it is to be human ... just as happens when we fall in love with someone.*

[LS 12]

It is more than information, the Pope is saying regarding St Francis's teaching, it is beyond head-knowledge – rather a delighted grasping by the heart. The reality of being in love with nature lies at the very heart of an ecological spirituality. Love inspires us and impels us to take action. Guilt is a poor motivator for improving our behaviour. In his universally acclaimed *The Universe is a Green Dragon* physicist Brian Swimme reminds us that it is by attraction, not by fear, that the human heart is unlocked. It is by allurement, that all-pervasive unconscious desire for one-ness, that the whole of creation is drawn, driven and sustained.

'Beyond the language of mathematics and biology ...', the Pope writes, referring, in part, to the sacramental language of poetry and the arts. This language opens our hearts with their play and their pain, their courage and their fear, their delight in life and their unending loneliness. In the 19th century Matthew Arnold wrote in his essay 'The Study of Poetry', 'More and more, humanity will discover that we have to turn to poetry to interpret life for us, to console us, to sustain us. Without poetry our science will appear incomplete; and most of what now passes for religion and philosophy will be replaced by poetry.' Traditionally, western Christian theology has been predominantly concerned with the understanding of God through conceptual and rational terms. These are, of course, vital in our attempts to grasp the mystery better intellectually, but a purely prose-based theology is an impoverished one.

Theology is about the human heart as well as the human mind. Deep within us, we humans have an intuitive sense of the Creator God, and this sense is usually expressed more clearly and experienced more fully through the arts and other non-verbal modes of creative imagination. All true artists strive to capture that which is at the core of humanity, be it called truth, goodness, beauty or life's meaning. A genuine work of art – poem, film, dance, music – has the power to evoke in people feelings of awareness of the Holy that are innate in everyone. At this precise moment we are lifted out of ourselves, time seems to stand still and we seem to be at one with everything. In this non-rational instant of knowing, our normal intellectual efforts, essential as they are, are transcended.

Pope Francis knows this. That is why he draws analogies and metaphors for the actual experience of God's presence from the world's best artists, past and present. His *Laudato Si'* is a clear example of that. To earth this heavenly awareness within us, he even reaches for the very common, but uniquely moving human experience when he writes 'just as happens when we fall in love with someone' (*LS* 11). Like art, the power of this particular moment conveys something of divine presence, and its beauty is seen as a felt reflection of the ultimate beauty we call God. Art and 'being in love' have the ability to expose the truth behind and within 'the ordinary'; they create the doorway to a religious experience, a heightened awareness of God's incarnate presence in the world. Pope St John Paul II states in his *Letter to Artists* (1999) that 'every genuine art form in its own way is a path to the inmost reality of humanity and the world. This reality is God. The world we live in needs such beauty to keep despair at bay ... It is beauty, like truth, which makes the invisible world palpable, and brings joy to the human heart.' It takes us beyond who and where we are. Without stimulating our faith-imagination this healing breakthrough will be a bridge too far.

It is for this reason that Pope Francis reminds us of his namesake's passion for revealing the message of Incarnation to all he met. 'Beyond the language of mathematics and biology', St Francis invites us 'to see nature as a magnificent book in which God speaks to us and grants to us a glimpse of his infinite beauty and goodness' (*LS* 11). Unlike so many who have gone before him, our Pope reaches for every possible teaching aid when it comes to revealing something of God. Whether it be the cycle of nature, the breathless moment of a sudden wonder, the extraordinary creations of artists in every medium and from any religion, he sees them as sacraments of disclosure, as precious vessels of grace. We are called to become aware of our normal and often shallow process of 'looking at' something rather than 'seeing into' it; of framing and pre-judging things as 'merely' secular or 'merely' human rather than allowing the surprise of our catching the deeper, unframed glimpse. Thus does the invisible become visible as we try daily to make the limitless Incarnation the measure of our understanding, our seeing and our very being.

## A FURTHER WORD

*Do we need to rediscover and embrace our graced imagination, to reawaken and nourish it, so as to make headway and heart-way in these new, alluring, often confusing but always rewarding insights about the links between Creation, Incarnation and evolution?*

'If Christianity is not only to survive but to flourish,' Delio says powerfully, 'it needs a new imagination for the earth community, a new dream for the cosmos, a new understanding of Christ in evolution as the mystery of the whole, which includes other religions, cultures, and the whole of the whole, and yes, other planets and forms of life. In short, Christianity needs a new direction, one pointing not upward but forward, not toward "heaven above" but to a new future of healthy relationships in the cosmos, a new heaven on earth, which is what Jesus prayed for ... Christianity must speak to the world of something new emerging from within, a new life, a new future, transcending the present world toward a deepened, more fruitful way of living ... As we evolve toward a new level of religious consciousness, we must let go of the past and engage the future, because the future is upon us. Without engagement toward new reality, Christ cannot come to be.'[34]

Our perennial quest is to discover the divine in the depths of matter, to be blessed with the grace of imagination and recognition. Ursula King explores the vision of Teilhard de Chardin. 'The concrete tangibility of the earth, the fragility of the living world, the haunting beauty of nature – all these were for Teilhard potentially a means for divine disclosure. The human experience of the senses – of seeing, touching, and feeling – could reveal a path leading to the "heart of reality," to God. Teilhard possessed an extraordinary sense of physical concreteness, of the strength and revelatory power of all created things in this world. He also felt a great yearning for a deeper unity of all things, with all their diversity ultimately held together by God.

... [The discovery of evolution] tore apart the rigid divisions of the traditional dualism between matter and spirit by making [Teilhard] realize that these were not two separate things, but two aspects of one and the same reality. Not identical or fused together, but one leading to the other, blazing matter disclosing the fire of spirit. This gave him an immense sense of release, a great thrill and feeling of inner expansion. With extraordinary insight, sensitivity, and great lyrical beauty he praised the spiritual power of matter, flood of energy, and crucible of spirit.

' ... He spoke of hallowed matter and hallowed life, of the holiness of evolution, and his Christian faith made him see the evolutionary stream of becoming, as God's creative action of which we are an integral part. Therefore we can find and commune with God through the earth and through life. By trusting life, by fully participating in and cooperating with it, we contribute to the building up of the body of Christ. This is a deeply sacramental and incarnational vision of the entire universe and of the significance of the human beings within it. It is also a deeply embodied spirituality with a profound reverence for all matter and life in their myriad forms.'[35]

# 6

## WE LIVE IN EACH OTHER'S SHADOW

*We need a conversation which includes everyone, since the environmental challenge we are undergoing, and its human roots, concern and affect us all. Any true ecological approach must become a social approach. 'Everyone's talents and involvement are needed to redress the damage caused by human abuse of God's creation.' (South African Bishops' Conference) [LS 14]*

'We need a conversation which includes everyone ... '. To what might the Pope be referring here? What kind of conversation and with what focus? In his writings he reveals a relentless belief in the sanctity of all things, of all creatures, of all people, of the whole cosmos. There are no exceptions to this vision. He is on fire with this deep compulsion about the presence of God everywhere. Spreading the joy of this good news is the constant motivation that drives his energy; it is constantly revealed in all he says and does. But his vision is too large, too ecumenical, too universal, too cosmic, too catholic, too challenging for entrenched believers. He begs us all to have '... big hearts, open to God'. And again, 'Let yours be great souls.' The 'magnanimity' (bigness) of God is one of his favourite refrains. And all of this bright vision springs from his theology, his spirituality, his understanding of Incarnation, his belief in the humanity of God.

To repeat, 'We need a conversation which includes everyone ...'. But a conversation about what? There are many opinions. Many thoughtful readers of *Laudato Si'* would now say that such a conversation would entail the search for a common ground to stand on, a clarification of people's understanding of the true heart of Christianity, the core of our teaching about Creation, Incarnation and the Church community. What needs explaining, for instance, is that everything we hold about Catholic teaching and worshipping and praying comes from one theology or another. Briefly, two theologies are referred to here. The more commonly taught and that best known to most Catholic Christians, is what is called the 'sin/redemption' theology. It believes that God's first plan for the Earth and human beings was shattered by the sin of Adam and Eve in a Garden of Eden. They (and we) were angrily banished from this haven of happiness, and we are still suffering, still involved in the terrible fallout from this out-of-time moment in a garden with two perfect specimens of humanity, a talking snake and a tempting apple. When myth is mistaken for history, when a story is read as reality, terrible consequences ensue. The flow of truth is disastrously distorted.

The punishment for the 'original sin' of our first parents, we are taught, is universally fierce. It cost us our intended happiness; it cost the world its perfection, it cost Jesus his life. We are still in this dark condition of sinfulness, begging God every day to forgive us because we are 'a guilty and damned mass', a *massa damnata*, as St Augustine put it. The world itself, our sins, our suffering and death are all the result, not of the divine river of natural evolution, but of this mythical original sin. There is a huge barrier between the Church and the world, between the sacred and the secular, between being human and being holy. These dark doctrines are still officially flowing through today's teaching Church. This is not the theology that Pope Francis teaches. Nor is it out of that context that he speaks to, and writes for us.

Now, a quick look at the other theology. It is, in fact, a most beautiful love story, utterly different from the sinister and grim one described above. Theologians, saints and scholars call this love story 'a theology of nature and grace', meaning that everything created is already holy, and was from the very beginning. It is also called 'a theology of Creation', which holds that there is no radical distinction, no separating line, no ultimate contradiction between Creation and God's grace, between the sacraments and our everyday experiences, between human love and divine love, human forgiveness and God's forgiveness. Why? Because of the Incarnation! 'The love with which we love each other,' preached St Augustine of Hippo in one of his sermons (285), 'is the same love with which God loves us.'

Unlike the baffling 'fall/redemption' model, with its punishing God who *could* stop the atrocities of the world but does not for his own reasons, this true and traditional (but forgotten, or supressed) theology holds that God, right from the beginning, desired to become human simply because, as St Thomas Aquinas and others believed, God's infinite love expressed itself first in Creation, and then finally and fully revealed in Incarnation. And that love is our essence too – recognised and revealed to a greater or lesser degree in all of us, and in the evolving world itself. (Think of the couple in love whose creative energy leads to a beautiful baby.) The love story went wrong when the myth was mistaken for fact. Paradise was not lost in the past; Adam and Eve never existed on this planet; the Creator's original blueprint for the universe and humanity was never destroyed by an actual 'fall'. The Pope hopes that this kind of 'new conversation in a new language' will surely change our wanton neglect of Mother Earth, who has lovingly, under God, provided our home, and will focus 'everyone's talents and involvement in redressing the damage caused by human abuse of God's Creation'. This radical theological shift is one dimension of the 'conversation' the Pope longs for. This shift will bring us a renewed perspective on the world and its preciousness, a deep and ancient human understanding of Creation.

## A FURTHER WORD

*There is an utterly new cosmic story, yet with seeds from a distant past. And there are Celtic spiritualities that are re-emerging at this time of unprecedented scientific progress. Are these phenomena part of the bigger picture the Pope is painting?*

'We are now restructuring our fundamental vision of the world,' says Brian Swimme. We are creating a new meaning for what we consider real, valuable, to be avoided or pursued. The new cosmic story

emerging into human awareness overwhelms all previous concep-
tions of the universe for the simple reason that it draws them all into
its comprehensive fullness. And most amazing of all is the way in
which this story, though it comes from the empirical scientific tradition, corroborates profound and surprising ways the ecological vision
of the Earth is celebrated in every traditional native spirituality of
every continent.'[36]

# 7

## OUR FORGETFULNESS – GOD'S DISAPPOINTMENT

*We need only take a frank look at the facts to see that our common home is falling into serious disrepair ... 'If we scan the regions of our planet, we immediately see that humanity has disappointed God's expectations'. [LS 61]*

The Pope wonders why we allow our common home to fall into serious disrepair and utter neglect. He also asks why we consciously and deliberately ignore her needs, abuse her callously, even destroy her in our ignorant greed. Does not our faith infuse us with a great obligation of care and concern for our Mother Earth? Is not Christianity created around the belief that God's own essential love is revealed and becomes available in every created reality? Does not the doctrine of Incarnation insist that Creation itself, and all of us too, *are* actually God's body? Of course it does. But we have forgotten the story. Or we deny it. As we have just seen, a disastrous doctrine about a mythical Adam and Eve whose original sin resulted in a 'fallen' world has turned many hearts against the holiness of the Earth from the start.

Pope Francis is trying to re-tell that corrupted story in the context of love. It will take a long time. The flawed theology that is leading to the disintegration of the Roman Catholic institution has infiltrated the organisation and system for so many centuries. But the Pope has the blessed power and energy of the peoples of the Earth behind him. Christians, of all people, should know that we revere the earth because it is God's child, God's evolving body, God's dream made visible. And in creating the world, and the trillions of galaxies with their trillions of planets around it, God took the huge risk of it all going wrong. That is the touching vulnerability of the divine heart at the core of Incarnation. Creation is God living dangerously! In 'Making', the poet R. S. Thomas pictures a restless God pausing on the fifth day while creating the world. Something beautiful is still missing. Beyond an obedient Creation, divine love must finally risk making a human creature who is free to return the love – or not.

> ... Yet still an absence
> Disturbed me. I slept and dreamed
> Of a likeness, fashioning it,
> When I woke, to a slow
> Music; in love with it
> For itself, giving it freedom
> To love me, risking the disappointment[37]

From where does that disappointment come? What seduces us from the true light? The Pope is not afraid to talk about the human sin of 'sloth', of not caring, of our refusal to value the principle of 'the common good'. He speaks of a chilling 'Power of Darkness'. At the 2015 Synod on the Family he warned: 'The Evil One is hidden; he comes with his very educated friends, knocks at the door, asks for permission to come in, lives with that person, and, drop by drop, anaesthetises his conscience'. Only eternal vigilance, he said, will notice the seduction. Richard Rohr reminds us that the very openness that can lead us into intimacy with an utterly free God who invites our cooperation and participation can also allow us to resist, oppose or deny Love. We are free to cling to our own egotistical resources, to climb proudly instead of descending humbly. We forget about disappointing God in our consumer culture where even spirituality can become consumerist too; our lives become a matter of personal success by adding on things rather than stripping ourselves of them, by attaining, achieving and performing – all of which pander to the ego. But, in fact, the abundant life is much more about letting go – of just about everything, including all of our negative judgements and thoughts, and our innate compulsion for acquisition and individual survival.

But we must fall before we can fly, before we can become painfully aware of our small horizons of self-preservation, of transcending the false in the recognition of the true. Meister Eckhart said, 'God is not found in the soul by adding anything, but by a process of subtraction.' This letting go of what is untrue, this shedding of what is called 'the false self', this discernment of what is truly authentic in our hearts, is the vision and work of Christianity. In a wonderfully thought-provoking statement Richard Rohr declared, 'I think the one and single purpose of religion is to lead you to an experience of your True Self in God. Every sacrament, every bible, every church-service, every hymn and doctrine, every bit of priesthood or liturgy is, as far as I'm concerned, for one purpose – to allow you to experience your True Self, who you are in God and who God is in you.'[38]

## A FURTHER WORD

*So why do we disappoint God? Is the world too busy, too distracted? What dimensions of Christianity will grab the attention of secular society today? And what teachings are utterly irrelevant to it?*

'In the matter of beliefs, in a secular age,' writes scientist and priest William Joseph, 'original sin has been a major influence in Christian thinking, and much more than most of us realize. This is the focus of the second and third chapters of the first book of the Bible, Genesis. According to one account, original sin is the reason we need to be "saved." It is the cause of our fallen nature. It is why humans die. But this whole emphasis makes little sense to the secular mind. It just doesn't match what happens in the real, educated world.'[39]

According to Joseph, no contemporary concept of Creation can accommodate original sin. In 2011 Jack Mahoney SJ wrote in *Christianity in Evolution*, 'It would be more theologically appropriate now to drop it [original sin] as unnecessary and cumbersome religious baggage.'[40] In 1947, Teilhard de Chardin said in *Christianity and Evolution;*

'It is no exaggeration to say that, in the form in which it is still commonly presented today, original sin is at the moment one of the chief obstacles that stands in the way of the intensive and extensive progress of Christian thought.' He also referred to it as, 'an embarrassment and stumbling-block'.[41] It is a stumbling block when we see God as other to the world, not as the inner, dynamic of the world, as the work of the Holy Spirit. 'To see the world from within God, is to see the world in its wholeness, in its unity', writes Ilia Delio. ' ... God is conceivable only within the context of evolution ... But if the story of evolution is the story of God, then we have a problem, because in this story there is no original perfection or Garden of Eden from which humans fell into sin. Rather it is a wild, unpredictable and unruly universe in which God emerges in the human person, Jesus of Nazareth.'[42]

# 8

## TO BE SPECIALLY CHOSEN

*Those who are committed to defending human dignity can find in the Christian faith the deepest reasons for this commitment ... 'Before I formed you in the womb I knew you' (Jer 1: 5). We were conceived in the heart of God and for this reason 'each of us is the result of a thought of God. Each of us is willed, each of us is loved, each of us is necessary.'*
(Benedict XVI) [LS 65]

Pope Benedict's words, quoted by Pope Francis, are balm for the soul. They picture a God who loves us unconditionally, who created us out of pure desire for our presence, who has delighted in us from the very beginning, and that delight has never wavered. There was never any lessening of that extravagant love and tenderness, never any expulsion from a mythical garden. In fact, Richard Rohr assures us that 'there is nothing we can do or say to decrease God's excessive love for us'. We can refuse to believe that, we can deny it, but we cannot change it. Moreover, God's love for us does not depend on whether we are worthy, religious, or in 'the state of grace'. Baptised or not, sinners or not, we are all, always and equally, but specially, embraced by divine love. Ours is a God who always forgives, who does not fret about our sins, who never punishes in this life or in the next, who just cannot prevent the terrible atrocities of our society, but weeps powerlessly with us.

Herbert McCabe OP writes that 'God is helplessly and hopelessly in love with us. Whether we are sinners or not makes no difference to him. He is just waiting to welcome us with joy and love.'[43] Infected as many of us were, and still are, by a heretical image of an angry, punishing God, is it possible for us to believe Fr McCabe's healing statement? Rohr insists that God never changes his mind about us. He is simply always in love with us. What God does again and again is to change our minds about him. We are not forgiven because we confess our sins; we confess our sins because we are already forgiven.

Once and for all, in his birth, death and resurrection, Jesus the Christ has reconciled all people with their Creator God (Heb 7: 27; 9: 12; 10: 10). And we, now, in our Sacrament of Reconciliation, want to celebrate this unrepeatable Passover mercy by forgiving all others in our lives. That is really why we 'go to confession'. Assured of God's forgiveness already, we now endeavour to spread that peace in every way possible, both personally and universally. Neither McCabe nor Rohr takes sin lightly; but for them God's love is always at the heart of our weakness, our powerlessness, our constant vulnerability. And the Sacrament of Reconciliation enables us to forever remember that the irresistible divine love that transforms our hearts must always lead to our generous forgiveness of everyone in our own lives. That's the only 'penance' that matters, 'to fill up what is missing' in the one and only sacrifice of the forgiveness of Christ (Col 1: 24).

Speaking about Julian of Norwich at a General Audience (2010) Pope Benedict quoted from her *Revelations of Divine Love*: 'I saw with absolute certainty that God, even before creating us loved us, with a love that never failed and will never vanish. And in this love he did all his works, and in this love our life lasts for ever ... ' Everything depends on this trust in the extravagance of God's love enfleshed in us – the quality of the mercy Pope Francis called for during the Year of Mercy (2016). In his apostolic letter *Misericordia et Misera* he writes of the 'creativity and revolution of mercy', and the inner love that motivates and sustains it. It takes a deep-seated devotion and constant love to persevere in devoting ourselves to 'restoring to weak and vulnerable millions' the dignity of their birthright, created as they all are, in that sublime image of God. Without this intimacy with God, the impact of the 'corporal and spiritual works of mercy' that he urges will carry no love.

Most Catholics do not believe in an unconditionally loving God. The caricature of an angry Father, drummed into us in childhood, has burned a deadly suspicion into our minds. Such indoctrination (it has been called the 'spiritual abuse' of children) destroys the possibility of ever trusting such a terrible monstrosity. Small wonder that most Catholics still regard God with a hidden fear. For generations, the clouds of threats about hell and limbo and divine anger and retribution have savagely closed the pathways into God's loving, reaching heart. We become defined as 'bad', from the beginning, rather than as beloved. How do we comfort and reassure our suffering, disillusioned, drifting young and old Church members that they are not exiled sinners in a fallen world? No! They are, instead, our Mother-God's beloved children carrying a dream of unutterable beauty.

Why do we need to be converted to this sublime and (for most) new and radical understanding of our faith? Because it will transform our hearts. 'Those who are committed to defending human dignity can find in the Christian faith the deepest reasons for this commitment ...'. When we know the astonishing love story of our creation and evolution we develop a fierce determination to protect and defend each other, especially those who are suffering poverty in any way, and then to do everything possible for the well-being of this beautiful Earth where all is connected and held together by the leading strings of divine love and energy. Here again Pope Francis is re-emphasising a most wonderful picture of God's unconditional love, and his imaginative ways of cherishing us. He paints a picture of extreme, divine love that will never end. Its infinite depth is non-negotiable. 'You were conceived in the heart of God!' Why were we never told these tender things? That we're in there, cherished, at the very heart of the mystery – a kind of fourth member in the dance of the Blessed Trinity deep within our own hearts!

## A FURTHER WORD

*Pope Francis believes that their Christian faith will enable Catholics to find a commitment, a motivation and an energy to care and defend human dignity and the integrity*

*of Creation. Through his devotion to the Incarnation, Teil-*
*hard de Chardin perceived a 'blaze of fire in the midst of*
*matter'. Do those passionate words and images of his heart*
*touch the love in yours?*

'Teilhard celebrated the powers of love, love in the cosmos, love between woman and man, love between different members of the human family. He saw love and union as central to Christianity. The Christian God is above all a God of love who can ultimately only be reached through love. Teilhard dreamed of a humanity that forms one single body animated by one single heart. A great visionary of human unity, he ultimately saw the building of the human community as a spiritual task leading human hearts to the heart of God, a heart burning like a blaze of fire in the midst of matter and radiating energy through the entire universe, consecrated and made holy by the powers of love and creative union.' [44]

# 9

## THE EARTH NEEDS NO HELP FROM US TO EVOLVE PERFECTLY

*We are not God. The earth was here before us and was given to us … Nowadays we must forcefully reject the notion that our being, created in God's image and given domination over the earth, justifies absolute domination over other creatures. [LS 67]*

Murmurs of surprise punctuated the conversations of the scripture exegetes when the Pope questioned an 'incorrect' interpretation of Genesis 1: 28. He was anxious to rectify a mistaken understanding of the text and to emphasise its true meaning – that of 'right relations' between the Earth, its creatures, humanity and God. Domination does not mean exploitation. 'The earth is the Lord's …' (Ps 24). '"The land is mine," said the Lord …' (Lev 25). All is gift; all is grace. We do not live in a holy meritocracy. We do not deserve the earth, or its fruits. We cannot merit it, earn it, bargain for it. The grateful heart delightedly and humbly accepts the abundance as pure gift. All creatures are a free blessing on us. But they also exist in their own right as small sacraments of God's amazing care and affection. The Pope reminds us that 'we are called to recognise that other living beings have a value of their own in God's eyes: 'By their mere existence they bless him and give him glory'. Where other creatures are concerned we now speak of 'the priority of *being* over that of *being useful'*. (German Bishops' Conference in *LS* 69)

It is such a blessing and a challenge to have a pope who is committed, with a passion, to the immense responsibility we humans have to care for the Earth, our home and God's incarnate dwelling place. Yet there are so many who will not be convinced of the truth of this threat. They stay wilfully blind to the clear scientific evidence of the devastation that is happening. Pope St John Paul II lamented this truth in 2001. 'Mankind, especially in our time, has, without hesitation devastated wooded plains and valleys, polluted waters, disfigured the earth's habitat, made the air unbreathable, disturbed the hydrogeological and atmospheric spheres, turned luxurious areas into deserts, and undertaken forms of unrestrained industrialisation, humiliating the flower-garden of the universe to use the image of Dante Alighieri in *Paradiso* XXII, 151.'[45]

Richard Rohr writes, 'Climate change and its effects – unpredictable, changing patterns of drought, flooding and powerful storms – are upon us. We have no time to lose. So many people and creatures will suffer and face extinction if we do not quickly change our lifestyle. Let us work together to creatively find solutions, to reduce our carbon footprint, to live more simply and sustainably on this, our only home. Humanity and the earth will really live or die together. The heart of the planet and our continued existence depend upon our choices and actions.'[46] Further on in his encyclical (*LS* 86) Pope Francis quotes the *Catechism of the Catholic Church*: 'God wills the interdependence of creatures. The sun and the moon, the cedar and the little flower, the eagle and the sparrow: the spectacle of their countless diversities, and tells us that no creature is self-sufficient. Creatures exist only in dependence on each other, to complete each other, in the service of each other.'(340)

He offers it as a truth to be meditated upon. He wants us to know, remember, internalise and contemplate that everything is connected, interwoven, interdependent. We are all responsible to everyone for everything. Tread on a daisy and trouble a star. The butterfly's wing here and the storm at the other end of the earth. The delicate interplay between insects, flowers, planets – everything. The fragile balance of the complex web of life so that nature can thrive. 'What I call my body,' wrote Teilhard de Chardin, 'is not part of the universe which I possess totally; it is the whole universe which I possess partially'. When asked if he believed in God, psychologist Carl Jung said, 'I could not say I believe. I know.' He had the experience of being gripped by something stronger than himself, something that people call 'God'. He saw the divine in the 'whole-making' energy of the soul, calling out 'Become who you are. Become all that you are: the whole of creation is within you.' Your infancy goes back a long way! Theologian Karl Barth reminds us that the same light at the core Creation shone in the eyes of Jesus – and still shines in all of us. German mystic Fr Angelus Silesius wrote, 'The rose which here on earth is now perceived by me, has blossomed thus in God for all eternity.'[47]

And again, it is only when we embrace a theology of Creation, and deepen and broaden our understanding of both the personal and cosmic role of Jesus, that we will ever have the respect and reverence for all of Creation that the Pope yearns for. There is a most alluring way of perceiving the presence and revelation of our Saviour in both the Christian story and the New Universe story. (To offer further insights into this mystery is the main aim of each Reflection's 'A Further Word'.)

## A FURTHER WORD

*All of this is an amazing new way of perceiving the role, presence and revelation of Jesus in both the Christian story and the New Universe story. Is there another way of putting it for those of us who are struggling to understand?*

According to Ilia Delio, 'Jesus ushers in a whole new understanding of heaven and earth. No longer is God reigning from a distance over ancient celestial domes. Now God is present in history, in the everyday world of life. Looking back from our own time we can say that the purpose of evolution appears in the life of Jesus Christ ... [And] Jesus' entire life points toward a new future in God.'[48] Here are some more striking insights to be grasped thoroughly through quiet meditation. There is a newness afoot, a promise of simple abundance in a new creation right here and right now, a vision of a movement towards a new and fuller future, a delightful way of seeing and of being and of loving. 'Christianity,' Delio continues, 'is not about salvation as an end in itself, or heaven, or eternal life – but new life now. It is about the fulfilment of promise and hope for a new creation. Although the direction of Christianity is forward movement, we have turned Christianity into historical nostalgia for something lost in the past. It has become backward-looking, a remembrance of things lodged in the seemingly glorious days of Christendom. We have lost sight of Jesus emerging in history as announcing something new, a new way of being for a new world, a new Big Bang, a new relatedness for a whole new future ... Earth is not a training ground for heaven. It is, rather, the very place where heaven unfolds ... Heaven, therefore, is not another world but this world clearly seen.'[49]

# 10

## EVERYTHING ON EARTH IS KISSED BY GOD

*'Each creature possesses its own particular goodness and per-fection ... Each of the various creatures, willed in its own be-ing, reflects in its own way a ray of God's infinite wisdom and goodness. We must therefore respect the particular goodness of every creature so as to avoid a disordered use of things'*
*(Catechism of the Catholic Church).* [LS 69]

'[In] God's loving plan,' writes Pope Francis, 'every creature has its own value and significance. In our time the Church does not simply state that other creatures are completely subordinated to the good of human beings, as if they have no worth in themselves, and can be treated as we wish.' And again, 'Even the fleeting life of the least of beings is the object of God's love.' Not every aspect of evolution reaches towards fulfilment in human beings. Creation has many goals within its unfolding. Humanity is one of them. This is emphasised by Pope Francis to clarify the reasons for our 'environmental conversion'. So it may not just be a matter of 'respecting the original goodness of every creature', but of acknowledging their wisdom and their grace of natural worship. Theologian Elizabeth Johnson took the title for her wonderful book *Ask the Beasts* from the Hebrew scriptures:

> If you would learn more, ask the cattle;
> Seek information from the birds of the air.
> The creeping things of earth will give you lessons,
> And the fishes of the seas will tell you all.
> There is not a single creature that does not know
> That everything is of God's making.
> God holds in power the soul of every living thing,
> And the breath of every human body. (Job 12:7–10)

Jesus commands that the gospel be preached 'to all Creation'. The Pope quotes St Francis about preaching to the birds 'just as if they were endowed with reason'. And in some sense they are, for each of them is indwelt with infinite intimacy by the Logos, who is 'the risen Christ who embraces and illuminates all things'. Many are surprised to realise that divine redemption stretches out beyond the salvation of individual, separate souls. 'All creatures are moving forward with us and through us towards a common point of arrival which is God.' It means that all our sisters and brothers in nature belong with us in the family of our Divine Parent.

The theology of Creation in *Laudato Si'* is in profound continuity with that which underpins *Evangelii Gaudium* (2013) and *Misercordiae Vultus* (2016) – about the immeasurable abundance of God's mercy. 'Not one sparrow is forgotten before God'. But *we* have forgotten. The environmental theologian Carmody Grey reminds us that Dostoyevsky believed that we should ask forgiveness of the birds; and Isaac the Syrian urged us to pray for reptiles. How much more should we pray for *all* creatures, on whom we are mutually dependent? Julian of Norwich believed that, because they are sustained by God's love in this life, they will live on in that love in heaven too. Who will help us with liturgies of light and depth to interiorise, identify with and celebrate these truths?

The world is a sacred and divine body to which we have a sacred and divine responsibility. In a very clear and powerful address to the United Nations General Assembly Pope Francis emphasised that a respect for the rights and intrinsic truth of the environment is based on two undeniable reasons. 'First, because we human beings are part of the environment. We live in communion with it, since the environment itself entails ethical limits which human activity must acknowledge and respect. Man, for all his remarkable gifts, which "are signs of a uniqueness which transcends the spheres of physics and biology" (*LS* 81), is at the same time part of these spheres. He possesses a body shaped by the physical, chemical and biological elements, and can only survive if the ecological environment is favourable. Any harm done to the environment, therefore, is harm done to humanity'. 'How did we miss that?' Rohr asks, when God's plan is clearly social, historical and universal, much more than the individualistic model of personal salvation that most of us grew up with.

' ... because every creature, particularly a living creature, has an intrinsic value, in its existence, its life, its beauty and its inter-dependence with other creatures. We Christians, together with the other monotheistic religions, believe that the universe is the fruit of a loving decision by the Creator, who permits man respectfully to use creation for the good of his fellow-men and for the glory of the Creator; he is not authorised to abuse it, much less to destroy it. In all world religions, the environment is a fundamental good.'[50]

## A FURTHER WORD

*For those of us who feel the attraction of beginning to live our Christian faith in a way that is radically influenced and enriched by the New Universe Story, there is a deep need to understand better something of the intrinsic inter-connectedness and interdependence of all creation.*

Remember, at your baptism you were called to prophesy. You have an undeniable inner authority springing from the presence of the Holy Spirit deep within you. Explore confidently. You are lovingly led. One of the emphases in this reflection is that we all flow from a single source, the heart of God, and what each of us does affects everyone else on the planet. Every choice we make liberates or diminishes others. Once we are deeply aware of the basic principle of this univer-sal interrelatedness, our choices will be more loving and the energy of compassion will flow stronger. We are playing our part within the process of evolution and the building of a more human, whole and holy community. We are co-creating a new world with God.

Evolution is a process of moving towards a more complex life, to a greater degree of relatedness, consciousness and deeper union. It is about attraction, union and emergence by which new things are formed. The Spirit of God is seeking to create a newness in our lives, calling us to a fresh wholeness that requires much letting go of what we have known, and co-creating with God an undreamt-of future for our Church, for our world and for ourselves. This does not mean forgetting the past, which has brought us to the present. The gospel life is about a new future in God. In an incarnational, evolutionary universe nothing is complete and God is still creating. We are a central part of this new creation, which is happening in our midst. The power within is the power of divine love incarnate which we call the Holy Spirit. We cannot really separate God from God's Creation. God is the source of all that is, the truth of reality itself, and that is the eternal fountain of love that far surpasses anything we could ever imagine or grasp. Vatican II, Pope Francis and our best theologians keep reminding us that Christianity is an evolutionary religion, empowered by its incarnational basis and beliefs.

# 11

## 'THE LOVE THAT MOVES THE SUN AND STARS'

*The mystery of the universe is love. Creation is of the order of love. God's love is the fundamental moving force in all created things: 'For you love all things that exist, for you would not have made anything if you had hated it.' (Wis 11: 24) Every creature is thus the object of the Father's tenderness, who gives it its place in the world. Even the fleeting life of the least of beings is the object of his love, and in its few seconds of existence God enfolds it with affection. Dante Alighieri spoke of 'the love that moves the sun and stars' [LS 77].*

Isn't this breathtakingly attractive language? How can we read and believe it, and yet remain the same? It is too beautiful, too deep, too tender to take in all at once. What does Pope Francis mean by the 'order of love'? What he means is extraordinary! Love is the vital, connecting, sustaining, empowering force of all beings and all creatures and all things, for every second of their existence – whether the mayfly during its 30 minutes with us or the dinosaur during its 200 years of living. Try to remember this every time you look around you; every time you use your senses; especially when times are hard, and you do not actually feel much love where you happen to be. Try also to explore this statement – that energy itself is the movement of love. Become more conscious of this revelation regarding your own doubts about divine presence always and everywhere, even in and through what we call death itself, including the fleeting lives of stillborn babies, the tragic and abrupt ending of those who take their own lives.

American writer and naturalist Wendell Berry believes that 'the world was created and approved by love, that it subsists, coheres, and endures by love, and that, in so far as it is redeemable, it can be redeemed only by love. I believe that divine love, incarnate and indwelling in the world, summons the world always toward wholeness ... '.[51] All creatures are woven into one community by the common thread of God's life, participating equally in the dynamism of divine being. 'Love is the very nature and shape of being,' writes Rohr. 'It is the essential energy of the entire universe from orbiting protons and neutrons to the orbiting of planets and stars.'

Teilhard de Chardin believed that love is the one, essential and constant influence in this unfolding. It is the energy that empowers the process. It permeates the whole universe. 'Driven by the forces of love, the fragments of the world seek each other so that the world may come to being ... the love of Christ is an energy into which all the chosen elements of creation are fused without losing their identity'.[52] Ilia Delio emphasises the role of the loving cooperation we all play in the evolving and developing universe. She quotes de Chardin: 'God evolves the universe and brings it to its completion through the instrumentality of human beings ... to love God we must also love what God loves. We are called to love this created world as God loves it ... We are to help transform this universe in Christ by seeing him in the universe, and by loving Christ at the heart of the universe.'[53]

Brian Swimme wrote his beautiful little book *The Universe is a Green Dragon* to honour his good friend, geologist Thomas Berry. They both use the lovely word 'allurement' a lot. They see it as Pope Francis sees the word 'attraction', and the phrase 'the order of love'. Everything, they are saying, is created by love. Elaborating on this insight, Swimme writes, 'This primal dynamism awakes communities of atoms, galaxies, stars, families, nations, persons, ecosystems, oceans and stellar systems. Love ignites being and, without it, all interest, enchantment, fascination, mystery and wonder would fall away, and with their absence all human groups would lose their binding energy'. 'And what is our fullest destiny?' he asks Berry. 'To become love in human form,' he replies.[54] Earlier in their conversation Berry suddenly says to Swimme, 'You scientists have this stupendous story of the universe. It breaks outside all previous cosmologies. But as long as you persist in understanding it solely from a quantitative mode you fail to appreciate its significance. You fail to hear its music. That's what the spiritual traditions can provide. Tell the story, but tell it with a feel for its music.'[55]

Beyond a great wonder at the extraordinary revelations of the birth and evolution of humanity and of the universe, what are the implications for our deepest soul? James Finley writes, ' ... what is truest is that we are all called to recognise, surrender to, and ultimately be identified with the mystery of God utterly beyond all concepts, all words, all designations whatsoever ... What's more, we are to realise that this boundless, birth-less, deathless mystery of God is manifesting itself, and giving itself to us completely in every breath and heartbeat ... If we could really experience all of that, as we sit here right now, just the way we are, we would experience God loving us into our chair, loving us into the present moment, breath by breath, heartbeat by heartbeat. And we would then bear witness to that realisation by the way we treat ourselves, the way we treat others, we way we treat all living things. This is the way; this is the great way ...'.[56]

## A FURTHER WORD

*Once we see Love itself as the power and energy that drives the universe on its way, and once we identify the source of life and growth and evolution as the creative work and play of the Holy Spirit, then the meaning of our faith and our deepest spirituality and worship cannot but be radically transformed. In all of this is there a danger of losing something precious from the past or are we building something more beautiful on it?*

Our faith must develop in tune with the rapidly evolving wisdom of science and theology. To freeze everything according to past doctrines and their fixed definitions is to watch our faith grow stagnant and die. And so do our hearts, and the light in our eyes. In this reflection Ilia Delio urges us to wake up, to stretch our thinking regarding all these beliefs, revelations and mysteries as we start a new journey, a new adventure in the faith. As an example, she takes our central notion of salvation. Most people, she says, would associate salvation with Jesus' death on the cross. If we expand our thinking from there to reflect about salvation in terms of the evolutionary universe, then salvation moves beyond the notion of 'Jesus saving me from sin'. We are inspired to see God's love at the heart of the cosmos, a love that heals, makes whole and generates new life. This love is visibly expressed in the cross of Jesus Christ. As we are healed and made whole by God's love, we, in turn, can promote greater wholeness in our communities and parishes in our world. This does not negate sin but puts it within the wider context of the whole cosmos. Beyond any personal failures and weaknesses, salvation is about a healing wholeness for all creation. 'Sin,' Delio said in an interview in 2016, 'is living in unrelatedness, disconnected from the whole.' Christ does not save us from the world; he is the reason *for* the world, he *is* the beating heart of the world.

Love radically changes us, and everything around us. Do we believe that, do we practise it, do we become it? Do we realise the power to transform, to fascinate, that we all carry – but mostly don't believe it?

Brian Swimme tells us, 'You will carry within yourself the complexity of the world in a manner unimaginable to your previous self. You will know that you are not disconnected from the life of the world, nor from struggling humanity in all its difficulties throughout the planet. You will learn the first glimmer of the profound manner in which humans bind together the entire social order through a heightened awareness of what is means to be a compassionate human ... [And then] we strive to fascinate. We work to enchant others. We work to ignite life, to evoke presence, to enhance the unfolding of being. All of this is the actuality of love. We strive to fascinate so that we can bring forth what might otherwise disappear. But that is exactly what love does; Love *is* the activity of evoking being, of enhancing life.'[57]

# 12

## THE HOLY SPIRIT IS THE LOVE-ENERGY OF A TURNING WORLD

*Creating a world in need of development, God in some way sought to limit himself in such a way that many of the things we think of as evils, dangers or sources of suffering, are in reality part of the pains of childbirth which he uses to draw us into the act of cooperation with the Creator. God is intimately present to each being, without impinging on the autonomy of his creature and this gives rise to the rightful autonomy of earthly affairs. His divine presence 'continues the work of creation'. (Vatican II) [LS 80]*

This is Pope Francis's way of talking about evolution. He refers to 'creating a world in need of development' and says, 'his divine presence continues the work of creation'. It is of fundamental importance that we reach some understanding of how this 'world development', this 'continuation of creation', this 'divine presence' and the 'autonomy of creatures' occurs. The Pope is also writing about God's guidance of evolutionary development, offering a word about 'the things we think of as evils, dangers or sources of suffering'. This extract contains mountains of mystery that need to be explored regarding the source of evil and the phenomenon of sin, especially now when the Adam and Eve story is no longer seen as an 'explanation' for these huge issues but is understood as the universal myth it is.[58]

'[God's] divine presence continues the work of creation.' Pope Francis is trying to help us to understand his own insights into the wonderful mystery of how God and Creation, the Holy Spirit and evolution, can sing harmoniously together. Far from being in competition with the laws of nature acting around us, the hand of God empowers the cosmos as it evolves. Theologian Elizabeth Johnson's

*Ask the Beasts: Darwin and the God of Love* seeks an understanding of faith that embraces the remarkable findings of science. In it she writes that 'the world evolves in an economy of divine superabundance, gifted with its own freedom, and in and through which the Creator Spirit's gracious purpose is accomplished.'[59] It may well be that our future lies not so much in an invisible heaven outside time, but in this world clearly understood, fully lived through and transformed by love. 'Earth is a physical place of extravagant dynamism that bodies forth the gracious presence of God', writes Johnson. 'In its own way it is a sacrament and a revelation ... The creating God, as the sustaining power and goal of the evolving world, acts by empowering the process from within.'[60]

We struggle to understand much of this kind of thinking. Our old mind-sets have to be replaced by the startling new insights of scientists and theologians as held together by Pope Francis in his writings. What is called a 'paradigm shift' (a radical new awareness) is beginning to happen in questioning, open minds. New personal and cosmic images of God will be born in our hearts as we surrender to the Holy Spirit. In *The Emergent Christ* Ilia Delio is preparing for a transformation in our consciousness as the Church merges into the framework of a new cosmology. She quotes Teilhard de Chardin: 'Creation and Incarnation are two moments of the one act of God's self-giving love ... There is a deep compatibility between Christianity and evolution.' We repeat St Thomas Aquinas's warning that 'if we get Creation wrong we get God wrong.'

Christians are now called to a new level of consciousness about God's loving energy in the first 'Flaring Forth' (Big Bang) nearly 14 billion years ago, and in the subsequent process of evolution. Every particle of Creation is imbued with divine love-energy, and is an incarnate expression of God's own creativity. One fundamental concept raised by the Pope in this extract concerns the presence of evil and suffering. He links them with 'the pains of childbirth'. Is he saying that evil is intrinsic to evolution? That there could not be a world created in space and time, without suffering and death? And where does that leave our 'original sin' teachings? A radical revision of this almost incomprehensible doctrine will open up the sacred space for developing an authentic theology of evolution, and this will lead to an exciting and challenging breakthrough for Catholic theology today. Our imagination and faith are stretched with every new scientific discovery.

There are echoes of the Pope's remarks in de Chardin's *The Phenomenon of Man*. 'Statistically, at every degree of evolution, we find evil always and everywhere, forming and reforming implacably in us and around us.'[61] For the Christian this may mean that however divinely guided by the Holy Spirit evolution may be, it still has to be understood as a 'trial and error' process, a groping towards higher levels of consciousness in which there are many costly failures and severe losses. Several authors offer a clarification of the papal observation.

While emphasising that 'moral evils are the greatest tragedies', Joseph P. Provenzano and Richard W. Kropf argue that 'much of what humans consider to be physical "evils" (like death) must remain a real factor in evolution, and the human tragedies connected with them are inevitable and a necessary part of an ongoing creative process ... we can arrive at an understanding that is capable of explaining the coexistence of evil in the world with a God and a creation that are both essentially good. In order to do this we envision that the universe began in a disordered, unconscious state (however we may imagine that beginning ... ) The universe then evolved to produce intelligent, self-aware beings with the power to choose, and with all of the resulting implications of this power'.[62]

## A FURTHER WORD

*Why is the current challenge to deepen our faith radically really so necessary? 'To reject evolution is to reject God', is a tenet many of our Christian scientists hold. Is the 'old faith of our fathers' (and mothers) not sufficient any more?*

Ilia Delio tells us, 'In *Science and Christ* Teilhard de Chardin wrote that Christians should have no need to be afraid or shocked by the results of scientific research. "Science should not disturb our faith by its analyses. Rather it should help us to know God better." To reject evolution, in his view, is to reject God. He envisioned the evolutionary process as one moving toward evolution of consciousness and ultimately toward evolution of spirit, from the birth of mind to the birth of the whole Christ ... Christianity, in Teilhard's view, is nothing short of a daring adventure. We are not only to recognise evolution but make it continue in ourselves. Before, Christians thought they could attain God only by renouncing the world. Now we discover that we cannot be saved except through the universe and as a continuation of the universe. We must make our way to heaven *through* earth ... The world, in its deepest physical roots, is penetrated with Christ. We are to harness the energies of love for the forward movement of evolution toward the fullness of Christ. This means to live from the centre of the heart where love grows, and to reach out to the world with faith, hope and trust in God's incarnate presence'.[63]

If you dare to love be prepared to grieve. For some reason loving, creating and suffering are all sisters in the one family. This is true at both the personal and the general levels of evolution. The Pope is here attempting to offer an explanation for much of the pain in our hearts and in our evolving world. His words call for deep reflection. They challenge many of our traditional and devotional notions of 'atonement' and 'reparation'. No suffering is actually 'sent by God' or 'a punishment for sin'. Is there another way of looking at our suffering? Teilhard de Chardin's meditation may help us understand a little more about the transformation of individual and universal suffering into spiritual energy.

'A sounder view of the universe in which we are caught up, is now providing us with the beginning of an answer to this problem. We are realizing that within the vast process of arrangement from which life emerges, every success is necessarily paid for by a large percentage of failures. One cannot progress in being, without paying a mysterious tribute of tears, blood, and sin. It is hardly surprising, then, if all around us some shadows grow more dense at the same time as the light grows brighter: for, when we see it from this angle, suffering in all its forms and all its degrees is (at least to some extent) no more than a natural consequence of the movement by which we were brought into being.

'... And it is here that there comes into play its irreplaceable part, the astounding Christian revelation of a suffering which (provided it be accepted *in the right spirit*) can be transformed into an expression of love and a principle of union: suffering that is first treated as an enemy who has to be defeated; then suffering vigorously fought against to the bitter end; and yet at the same time suffering rationally accepted, and cordially welcomed, inasmuch as by forcing us out of our egocentrism and compensating for our errors, it can supercentre us upon God. Yes, indeed: suffering in obscurity, suffering with all its repulsiveness, elevated for the humblest of patients into a supremely active principle of universal humanization and divinization – such is seen to be at its peak the fantastic spiritual dynamic force, born of the cross.'[64]

'....In suffering, the ascending force of the world is concealed in a very intense form. The whole question is how to liberate it and give it a consciousness of its significance and potentialities. The world would leap high toward God if all the sick together were to turn their pain into a common desire that the kingdom of God should come to rapid fruition through the conquest and organization of the earth. All the sufferers of the earth joining their sufferings so that the world's pain might become a great and unique act of consciousness, elevation, and union. Would not this be one of the highest forms that the mysterious work of creation could take in our sight?[65]

# 13

## THE HOLY SPIRIT IS THE MIDWIFE OF OUR IN-NER BEAUTY

*The Spirit of God has filled the universe with possibilities and therefore, from the very heart of things, something new can always emerge: 'Nature is none other than a certain kind of art, God's art, impressed upon things, whereby those things are moved to a determinate end. It is as if a shipbuilder were able to give timbers the wherewithal to move themselves to take the form of a ship.' (St Thomas Aquinas) [LS 80]*

There are huge questions here that explore and examine our under-standing of God as Creator of the world. One particular issue, especially for Catholic Christians, is that of the process of evolution on the one hand, and the guiding presence of the divine Creator on the other. In the light of evolutionary reality, how can God still be the Creator of all things? When we reflect on the random nature of evolutionary development, with its hits and misses, its innumerable cul-de-sacs and variations, where can we point to the steady, accu-rate, guiding hand of God as we could definitively do before? How can both seemingly irreconcilable forces and drives be seamlessly combined? And, given the discussion space around these new and necessary questions about evolution in general, is there doctrinal cer-tainty about the separate creation of the human soul? We can only seek, reflect, read and meditate on such a wonderful mystery. And we do find writings and presentations that help us enormously when we come with open welcoming minds, eager to make intellectual sense of our faith.

In 2014 Pope Francis offered clarification at the Plenary Session of the Pontifical Academy of Sciences. 'When we read in Genesis the account of Creation,' he said, 'we risk imagining God as a *magus* [wizard], with a magic wand able to make everything. But it is not so. He created beings and allowed them to develop according to the internal laws that he gave to each one, so that they were able to develop and arrive at their own fullness of being. He gave autonomy to the beings of the Universe at the same time at which he assured them of his continuous presence, giving being to every reality. And so Creation continued for centuries and centuries, millennia and millennia, until it became that which we know today, precisely because God is not a demiurge of a conjurer, but the Creator who gives being to all things. The beginning of the world is not the work of chaos that owes its origin to another, but derives directly from a supreme Origin that creates out of love. The Big Bang, which nowadays is posited as the origin of the world, does not contradict the divine act of creating, but rather requires it. The evolution of nature does not contrast with the notion of Creation, as evolution presupposes the creation of beings that evolve.'[66]

It is important that we grapple with these issues if we hope to be caught up in delight and wonder at the unfolding mysteries of science and spirituality. We need to develop a profound interest, familiarity and fascination with these revelations. Opportunities for study and sharing, for both young and old must swiftly be made available. A central source of wisdom and understanding is priest, prophet and scientist Pierre Teilhard de Chardin, who helps us to grasp central aspects of the mystery. He saw the evolutionary process of Creation in the light of faith. It is the challenge facing all of us.

To be Christian is to be in evolution; and to be in evolution is, in the guiding words of another safe teacher, Ilia Delio, 'to live from the centre of the heart and to reach out to the world with faith, hope and trust in God's incarnate presence ... The Gospel of Jesus Christ is the living word of God that continues to be spoken as the word of evolution ...'. God creates and saves, you might say, through evolution. Delio writes of the shining of God *coming through* Creation, 'always radiating through a world that is gradually becoming transparent'. It is important that we understand that the Incarnation is not a one-off event in history: it holds the key to the true reality of all time and space, of all life and its religions, as it evolves and grows towards final fulfilment in the heart of God. It is, in fact, a long love story drawing us to cherish and transform our true earthly and cosmic home. In *Waiting for God* French philosopher Simone Weil wrote that 'the beauty of the world is Christ's tender smile for us coming through matter ... It is like a sacrament'.

Meanwhile, many Catholic readers will struggle with the inherent problem posed by the Pope in these last two extracts and reflections. 'How can evolution be self-determining without challenging God's role as ultimate Creator of everything?' It is a question that will reverberate in Catholic Christian circles for many a day. The Pope quotes St Thomas Aquinas's attempt to explain the matter. How could the shipbuilder's timbers sense their future role in a fine ship? Could they somehow 'feel' the allure of the sea? How do you understand it? It's an intriguing matter. It is at the heart of the Christian's grasp of evolution. Maybe writer and philosopher Antoine de St Exupéry, author of *The Little Prince*, unintentionally gives us a hint when he writes: 'If you want to build a ship, don't first drum up people to collect wood, and don't assign them tasks and duties; rather teach them to long for the endless immensity of the sea.'

## A FURTHER WORD

*Reading these words of the Pope, many will continue to ask, 'Is evolution, then, self-directed or God-directed?' We need all the help we can get with the question.*

Theologian Elizabeth Johnson faces the question in this way: 'Nature, it appears, bears a raw openness to the future. More than a sacrament of continuous divine presence, more than a locus of divine compassion, it is also the bearer of a divine promise. The living, ever-dawning God abides in the world most intimately in the mode of promise: "*Behold, I make all things new*" (Rev 21: 5). To sum up: an ecological theology (of creation) proposes that the Creator Spirit dwells at the heart of the natural world, graciously energising its evolution from within, compassionately holding all creatures in their finitude and death, and drawing the world forward toward an unimaginable future. Throughout the vast sweep of cosmic and biological evolution, the Spirit embraces the material root of life and its endless potential, empowering the cosmic process from within ... [Seeking] to make intelligible the idea that the Creator Spirit, as ground and sustaining power, and goal of the evolving world, acts by *empowering* the process from within. They see divine, creative activity *in, with and under* cosmic processes. God made the world, in other words, by empowering the world to make itself.'[67]

# 14

## 'AND HONOURED AMONG WAGONS I WAS PRINCE OF THE APPLE TOWNS ...'

*The history of our friendship with God is always linked to particular places which take on an intensely personal meaning; we all remember places, and revisiting those memories does us much good. [LS 84]*

You feel the Pope is enjoying reflecting on special sacramental moments of his life, both past and present. He dwells on the sacredness of all things, things that are sacred just by being themselves – animals, plants, insects, deserts, oceans, skies, planets, fleas. As well as human beings, who are created in God's image, every creature has its own purpose. Nothing is superfluous. God's extravagant love is inscribed into everything. There is something deeply touching in the evocative words and phrases he uses in this section: 'Soil, water, mountains – all that exists is a caress of God'. That is why, he writes, 'anyone who has grown up in the hills and fields, or who used to sit by the well to drink, or played outdoors in the streets or the neighbourhood square – going back to these places is a chance to recover something of their true selves'. When you have the time, try to recapture some of those places and moments when you felt, and still feel close to nature, when you sense a 'oneness', a connection with everything, with our common being. These special times of disclosure, of spiritual 'peak moments', of maybe fleeting and timeless experiences of 'otherness', of the numinous, are sacramental glimpses of our ineffably beautiful Mother-Creator – they last for ever because they touch eternity.

At home in the South-West of Ireland we lived in the shadow of the 'Two Paps Mountains' (Dhá Chíoch Danann), faithful companions during the seasons and decades of the lives of our family. Named in honour of the goddess Danu, they reminded us of those who went before us – the pagans, the Celts, the Christians – and of our common lineage and evolving understanding of God. It was at the request of the local people that I celebrated the Eucharist on the Paps one spring morning. The magic mist (ceo draíochta) of folklore parted and, with the inner, mystical eye of our faith, we sensed the bright presence of a mystery beyond us. It was a sacramental moment if ever there was one. Away to the west of us the Atlantic Ocean sang of God's vastness; to the east, the Golden Vale of Munster reflected God's extravagant bounty. High overhead, wandering across a perfect sky, a little family of stray clouds was a sacrament of humanity's lonely pilgrimage in search of home. All of us, I'm sure, in that sacred space, were connecting with unspoken, unspeakable dimensions of our being – another word for silent adoration. Maybe it was something like this the Pope had in mind when he pondered about the graces hidden in such places – the moments, the memories.

Some years ago (1988) we were celebrating the opening of our new and beautiful St Benedict's Church in Leeds, Yorkshire. To gather there in the darkness before the Easter dawn was, for us, a dream come true. The community's faith-story was moving into a new phase. Lest we might forget our humble beginning long before that unforgettable moment, Frank, a parishioner, took a portion of the old altar from the first church in Aberford and crafted hundreds of tiny crosses for people to take home – precious reminders, like 'sacraments of centuries', of a long infancy. Carefully, and with a small smile, he handed them round 'like bread and wine'. Later that evening, I wrote 'Aberford Cross':

> ... Smoothed and grained by human breasts
> at the holy moment of communion,
> each cross is still urgent with their secrets,
> with memories that bless and burn.
> So many tears in a piece of wood.

One last example of what the Pope may have meant by reminding us of the deeper meaning of those 'places we played in', experiences that we tend to return to, often at unexpected times – our childhood homes and streets and fields. The days and places of our youth become so special to us in later years. And in summertime, especially, we dream about them. The warm winds make us vulnerable to forgotten moments – and comfort our hearts. There is often an ache in us when we look back on our lives. Something of God is alive and well in us then. There is the glow of divinity in the immediacy, the 'full-on' attitude, the sense of excitement and openness that graces those years. Small wonder that Jesus reached for a child when they asked him for a role model. Jesus was as much God in his childhood as he was at the traumatic end of his life in his last week of pain and resurrection.

> Now I was young and easy under the apple boughs
> About the lilting house and happy as the grass was green,
> The night above the dingle starry,
> Time let me hail and climb
> Golden in the heydays of his eyes.
> And honoured among wagons, I was prince of the apple towns[68]

## A FURTHER WORD

*The Pope believes that our friendship with God is usually 'linked to particular places which take on an intensely personal meaning'; that we all have a special 'place for grace', for an intimacy with divine beauty, with a 'thin' place, according to Celtic spirituality, where the heavens and the earth are very close to each other. Where is your place?*

For John O'Donohue one such place lay at the foot of Maumean, one of the Connemara mountains. He believed there was life, memory and a profound presence in the rocks and the hills there. In 'Connemara in

Our Mind' he painted a picture of the light and colour of his beloved landscape:

> In an instant
> the whole place flares
> in a glaze of pools,
> as if a kind of sun
> let a red net
> sink through the bog,
> reach down to a forgotten
> infancy of granite,
> and dredge up
> a haul of colours
> that play and sparkle
> through the smother of bog,
> pinks, yellows, amber and orange ...

(Excerpt from, 'Connemara in Our Mind,' by John O'Donohue)[69]

# 15

## Everything is a love letter from God

*God has written a precious book, 'whose letters are the multitude of created things present in the universe'. No creature is excluded from this manifestation of God. 'From panoramic vistas to the tiniest living form, nature is a constant source of wonder and awe. It is also a continuing revelation of the divine.' (Canadian Bishops' Conference) [LS 85]*

Notice what the Pope is saying here – that the first Creation is already a special story about God, a precious book in which every page, every creature, is a revelation of the divine Creator. He is saying that God was already in the world from the beginning of its existence, long before the coming of Jesus into our world at the first Christmas. He believes that Creation itself is a central part of the Christian story. It will be helpful for all of us to get a clearer glimpse of this revelation – that Creation itself is the first love letter from our Parent-God – the first Bible, the first glimpse of our divine Mother, her first incarnation. It is an insight we need to grasp if we are ever to be touched by what our Pope has in his heart for our enlightenment and nourishment. Once again, a summary.

The Incarnation of God did not only happen in Bethlehem 2000 years ago. The Incarnation actually began 14 billion years ago with a moment we now call 'The Big Bang'. The human incarnation of God in Jesus is comparatively recent, but, before that, in the original incarnation of the amazing story of evolution, God had already begun the mysterious process of becoming flesh by first becoming Creation itself. The first 'Happy Christmas', you could say, was uttered in the 'flaring forth' of the Big Bang. It may take us some time to truly get our heads around these teachings because many of us were brought up with a deeply flawed doctrine of an 'original sin' committed by

Adam and Eve, followed by God's angry demand for the sacrifice of his Son, because we too, were/are guilty, all of us being somehow complicit in that first sin that ruined everything. But we were never told about another story – the true one. How do we explain this terrible omission? There are many reasons. It's a long story that I will attempt to clarify. It is also a terrible tragedy.

Fall or no fall, the coming of the Messiah, the Saviour, was lovingly willed from the very beginning of time. 'Creation,' wrote St Thomas Aquinas, 'is the primary and most perfect revelation of the Divine ... If we do not understand Creation correctly, we cannot hope to understand God correctly'. Franciscans St Bonaventure and Blessed John Duns Scotus held that the whole of Creation was the necessary preparation for the divine Incarnation in Jesus, the Human One, the Son of Humanity. For Christians, the question about the divine intention for the Incarnation (Did Jesus come to atone for the sin of Adam and Eve, and that of all of us by complicity, or would he have come anyway?) is a crucial one with implications for the Church's basic theology of creation, of incarnation, of redemption, of Church and of the sacraments, and for every aspect of the Christian life, both personal and universal. Is there a theology, people ask, other than one based on a fall/redemption supposition, that tells a different story – a story of original grace and beauty rather than of original sin? (I have already touched on this in Reflection 6.)

By way of reply theologians point to two schools of theology that are central to our present reflection. One is the familiar sin/redemption model with its basic themes of atonement, reparation and sacrifice. God's first intention for humanity and the world (Plan A) failed, we were told, because of a sin by our First Parents in a garden called Eden. An angry God demanded the bloody sacrifice of his son Jesus to redeem us from hell (Plan B), but we are all still suffering the consequences of that epic act of primal disobedience as fallen creatures in a fallen world. Even babies need cleansing, exorcism, from this inherent evil. (Otherwise they were buried in remote and windswept, lonely and unconsecrated graves, condemned to a godless eternity alone, without God's company. It is hard to believe that most of us grew up believing all of this inhuman and loveless teaching. In fact our whole faith has been dominated by this negative, oppressive and mistaken teaching.)

The other model is called a theology of Creation, or a theology of nature and grace. Creation, our earth, our bodies, our death, all we mean by 'the natural', the 'secular', are not the unfortunate results of what Blessed John Henry Newman called 'some terrible aboriginal calamity'. On the contrary, they are already graced, and carefully fashioned in the divine image. God was as surely present in the world before the birth of Jesus as much as after it. (The very recent incarnation of God in Jesus is that unique event of the revelation in human flesh of the love and meaning in the whole story of Creation, that final, unambiguous and undeniable final unveiling, proclamation and guarantee of the divine intention from the very beginning.)

To be open enough to accept, believe and cherish all of these insights as true is often a bridge too far for many Catholic Christians. 'Acknowledging the intrinsic value and beauty of creation, the elements, plants and animals is a major paradigm shift for most Western and cultural Christians,' writes Richard Rohr. 'We limited God's love and salvation to our own human species and even then to only certain "chosen" people ... All you have to do today is walk outside and gaze at one leaf, long and lovingly, until you know, really know, that this leaf is a participation in the eternal being of God ... For a true contemplative (which we all fundamentally are), a falling green leaf will awaken awe and wonder just as much as a golden tabernacle in a cathedral.'[70]

## A FURTHER WORD

*The New Universe Story calls for an immense expansion of our incarnational theology. Incarnation confirms the divinity of not just the baby Jesus, or humanity in general, but of the whole cosmos, of all Creation. Why were we not told about these marvellous truths of our faith before now?*

There are many reasons. All of them without honour. Better left for another time. Theologian Elizabeth Johnson is trying to get us back on track: 'Given the interconnected character of the material world, the Christ event ramifies (branches) throughout the whole creation so that matter in all of its finitude and perishing is fundamentally blessed by being united to God in a new way. St Pope John Paul II (in his encyclical *Lord and Giver of Life*) explained this succinctly: "The Incarnation of God the Son signifies the taking up into unity with God not only of human nature, but in this human nature, in a sense, of everything that is flesh; the whole community, the entire visible and material world. The Incarnation then also has a cosmic significance, a cosmic dimension. The first-born of all creation, becoming incarnate in the individual humanity of Christ, unites himself in some way with the entire reality of humanity, and in this reality with all flesh, with the whole of creation" ... The incarnation, a densely specific expression of the love of God already poured out in creation, confers a new form of nearness to God on the whole of earthly reality in its corporal and material dimensions, on all of Earth's creatures, on the plants and animals, and on the cosmos in which planet Earth dynamically exists.'[71]

'God incarnates in the cosmos. He and his incarnations are inseparably connected with one another. He is not in his incarnation; He manifests himself as incarnation. He reveals himself in the tree as tree, in the animal as animal, in the person as person, in the angel as angel. They are not creatures in addition to which there is a God who slips into them. God is each and every one of these creations and yet is not them, since God never exhausts himself in any single creature, but is always all the others as well. It is precisely this that is the experience of the mystic. The mystic apprehends the cosmos as the meaningful manifestation of God.'[72]

# 16

## THE MUSIC 'IN THE BLAZE OF THE SUN AND THE FALL OF THE NIGHT'

*'To sense each creature singing the hymn of its existence is to live joyfully in God's hope and love' (Japanese Bishops' Conference). In contemplation of creation we see in each thing a teaching from God, 'for the believer, to contemplate creation is to hear a message, to listen to a silent voice'. There is a divine manifestation in the blaze of the sun and the fall of night. 'I express myself in expressing the world; in my effort to decipher the sacredness of the world, I explore my own.'*[73] [LS 85]

In this extract Pope Francis is seeing all Creation through the lens of a theology of Creation, of nature and grace. Unlike our common theology of sin/redemption, as we have seen, which separates the holy from the human, grace from nature, a theology based on the Incarnation sees all Creation as sacred. Notice the words of the Pope here, – 'in contemplation of creation we see in each thing a teaching from God'; 'God has written a precious book, whose letters are the multitude of created things present in the universe.' This is a very different story from the familiar and dismal one that indelibly, and from childhood, coloured our relationship with God – an indoctrination that blighted the roots of any subsequent possibility of falling in love with an unconditionally loving Mother Creator. Another word of explanation about this renewed, rediscovered and very beautiful theology of nature and grace may help at this stage.

An orthodox theology of Creation, the truly original, traditional but utterly neglected teaching of the Church, holds that God, right from the beginning, desired to become human simply because, as St Thomas Aquinas put it, infinite love needed to express itself outside itself – something like, as we have mentioned, the mutual love of a

couple being enfleshed, incarnated in their baby. This divine becoming, this expression of a great love (*bonum est sui diffusivum*) first
happened in Creation, and this sublime and cosmic moment of the
Big Bang was fully and definitively revealed much later in the Incarnation of God in Jesus. And by virtue of solidarity and derivation, this
love is embodied in all of us, and in the evolving world itself. That is
why we say that the story of evolution is the love story of God leading up to the birth of Christ – and beyond.

So, being human does not (as we were often told) mean being banished, fallen, cursed, as if God's original dream for us was, at some
stage, radically destroyed. The heart of the love story of creation is
broken, as we have noted earlier, when mythical truth is confused
with historical truth. Paradise was not lost in the past; Adam and Eve
never existed on this planet; nor was the Creator's original blueprint
of aching desire for us ever destroyed by an actual 'fall'. If all of this
is true – that the essential face of Creation, as we have it, has always
carried the tender look of love rather than the sinister shape of sin,
then other intrinsically connected issues to do with our understanding of faith will need urgent and radical revision.

Our faith-lives are shaped by our images of God. Beautiful experiences of the divine are possible only when we deeply imagine and
believe in a God of utter self-giving and astonishing love. 'You are
God's love-letters, written not with ink but with the love called the
Holy Spirit: not on tablets of stone but across the pages of your human
hearts' (2 Cor 3). The primary revelation of this intimacy is going on
since the Big Bang 13.7 billion years ago. Creation is the first Bible,
the 'precious book' referred to here by the Pope. 'Revelation comes
bound in two volumes,' wrote St Thomas Aquinas, 'the Book of Creation and the Book of Scripture'. God walks to us in two pairs of shoes,
you might say, the shoes of nature and the shoes of the man Jesus. The
French philosopher Paul Ricoeur tells of his intense relationship, even
unity, with the divine heart of the universe. Brother Carlo Carretto
also calls on the experiences of nature to express his sense of spiritual
awakening: 'The moment when God's love penetrated every corner of

my being and filtered through my being like sun through the leaves of a forest. I feel immersed in God like a drop in the ocean, like a star in the immensity of light, like a lark in the summer, like a fish in the sea. Most of all, like a child in its mother's lap.'[74]

All ground is holy ground. The land we stand on is sacred; we are connected to it and part of it. All we need, in our fretting and worrying, is to realise this truth, to be intensely aware of the connectedness of all things. It is in this connectedness to all things and creatures that we are connected to God. That is when we find a deep peace and freedom. Professor Sam Keen has written:

> When the moon rises in my blood, and suns are born and
> Burst in the atoms of my substance, and I am one body with
> the World, a profound joy fills the wells of my being.[75]

> And Welsh poet Dylan Thomas also expresses
> an inner affinity with nature (and, the Christian would say,
> with the Holy Spirit):

> The force that through the green fuse drives the flower
> Drives my green age ...
> The force that drives the water through the rocks
> Drives my red blood.[76]

## A FURTHER WORD

*How to be in the presence of the Presence – when the natural, human and divine flow as one within you. Beyond knowing about it, how do we experience something of this deeper intimacy?*

Brian Swimme tell us that we need to '[L]earn to listen. *Really* listen. The magnificent feelings of the universe flood you: listen for them in every situation in your life. Listen to your friends with such sensitivity that you are leeching the very air that surrounds you. When you leave your friend, her presence will emanate from you. Notice this, feel the presence radiating away from you ... When you walk into a forest learn to tremble with the magnitude of what are about ... Forests are alive with music on all sorts of hidden levels, and when you hear this music you will know that that the forest has permeated every cell of your body. The natural, human and divine worlds flow together into your feelings. You need no teacher. The universe is your teacher ... We are awash with the presence of the universe, already swamped in its beauty ...To live as a mature human being is to journey home, and our home is enchantment. We are the creative, scintillating, searing, healing flame of the awesome and enchanting universe.'[77]

# 17

## THE WONDER OF YOU – 'LIKE A NIGHT IN THE FOREST, LIKE A STORM IN THE DESERT'

*The universe as a whole, in all its manifold relationships, shows forth the inexhaustible riches of God. St Thomas Aquinas noted that multiplicity and variety 'come from the Creator who willed that what was wanting in one, in the representation of the divine goodness might be supplied by another, in as much as God's goodness could not be represented fittingly by any one creature.' Hence we need to grasp the meaning and variety of things in their multiple relationships [LS 86].*

Read the first sentence in this extract again. Pope Francis sees the universe as a whole, with all its relationships, as a revelation of the beauty and richness of God. He does this because of the Christian doctrine of Incarnation. He sees the astonishing revolution brought about by the Christmas baby. Most Catholics have not been helped to deeply understand this shocking good news. A new consciousness of the bigger picture is called for, a clearer insight into the intrinsic connection between Creation and Incarnation, into the developing conversation between the scientists and the theologians.

All of these conversations, reading and study are not just part of a cerebral game about ideas, theories and hypotheses; they are the solid foundations that add authenticity, clarity, resonance, wonder and deep affection to how we see God, how we understand Jesus, how we regard the Church with its teaching about sin, grace and redemption, how we live our daily lives, how we say our morning and evening prayers, how and why we help and protect our neighbour and the planet – and why we go to Mass on Sundays. A fundamental concept is that 'the universe as a whole, in all its multiple relationships', and ourselves as well, all flow from one source; some will call it the process of evolution; others, the delicate, personal, loving attention of the Holy Spirit.

Pope Francis is fond of quoting these particular words of St Thomas Aquinas about every created thing being necessary to give us a clearer picture of the nature of our Parent-God. This paragraph gives another welcome insight into the inseparable link between Creation and its Creator. Aquinas's original utterance in full is: 'God brought things into being in order that his goodness might be communicated to creatures, and be represented by them; and because his goodness could not adequately be represented by one creature alone, he produced many and diverse creatures. So that what was wanting to one in the representation of the divine goodness might be supplied by another. For goodness, which in God is simple and uniform, in creatures is manifold and divided.'[78]

Whatever reasons we may usually have for protecting the planet and all its inhabitants, including the tiniest of these, Aquinas's words provide the deepest motivation for doing so. Every single aspect of Creation is the individual and careful work of God, providing another window into the divine creativity, another expression of the divine face, another embrace of the divine heart. (Again, just as every child in a large family tells us something special, something different, about the parents.) When we wantonly destroy any seemingly unimportant, unnecessary part of Creation, we are closing a window, killing a vision, burning a small blueprint of the divine essence, getting rid for ever of an image of God.

But look at what is happening around us today. We are all complicit in a current and crazy destruction of this world and the beautiful treasures it carries. Small wonder our Pope is so anxious. He knows well that human activity is driving many of the planet's species dangerously close to extinction. According to a 2016 World Wildlife Fund/Zoological Society of London report, global vertebrate populations are likely to have declined by over 50 per cent on their 1970 levels before 2020. These are seen as extraordinary figures, suggesting that a mass extinction in the near future has become a serious danger. The report warns of a threat of multiple extinctions on a scale not seen since the dinosaurs left us. The report also explains that we are entering a new era in Earth's history, which is described as the Anthropocene era, when humans rather than natural forces will be the primary drivers of planetary change.

In his encyclical Pope Francis warns about the devastating effects of the deteriorating state of nature, not just in the destruction of the delicate balance and beauty of our global wildlife, but in the victimising of humans, particularly the poor, who are the last to contribute to this inhuman greed, and the first to suffer from the consequences. In the light of 20 known mass extinctions over a long span of evolution, each involving a striking contraction of species diversity, the Pope is the first to agree that a mass global wildlife conservation process, similar to the process begun in Kyoto in 1997 to combat climate change, is urgently required.

The good news in this threatening and depressing scenario is that the vast majority of species have not yet gone beyond the point of no return. A concerned editorial in the London *Times* (27 October 2016) believes that 'in the longer term (but not too much longer given that the overall rate of decrease is running at 2% a year), the best course of action for Earth's dominant species is for it to reproduce more slowly and make more efficient use of its own habitat ... After centuries of unfair, unequal genocidal struggles with human beings, the planet's other inhabitants deserve a long period of being left in peace.' *Laudato Si'* is a bright light in this consuming darkness.

## A FURTHER WORD

*Are we Christians, who, given our true Creation tradition and sacramental beliefs, should be the first to be concerned, to be deeply involved in committing ourselves to saving our Earth for the future, responding wholeheartedly to the Pope's plea? The least we can do is to continue to deepen our*

*consciousness of the mystery we are examining, to enter*
*into it with full hearts and willing minds.*

'[But] something tremendous is occurring in our time, something with the power to break up this impasse. I mean the radical transformation of our fundamental world-view as the cosmic story of our origins and development takes hold in human awareness. When I say "origins and development" I mean more than the human species. I mean the origin and development of the universe as a whole. We have discovered something with overwhelming possibilities. The universe can no longer be regarded as a result of a chance collision of materials, nor as a deterministic mechanism. The universe considered as a whole is more like a developing being. The universe has a beginning and is in the midst of its development: a vast cosmic *epigenesis* (process of evolutionary change). Everything that exists is involved in this emergence – galaxies and stars and planets and light and all living creatures ... Most amazing is the realisation that every thing that exists in the universe came from a common origin. And we are the first generation to live with an empirical view of the origin of the universe. We are the first humans to look into the night sky and see the birth of stars, the birth of galaxies, the birth of the cosmos as a whole. Our future as a species will be forged within this new story of the universe ...

' ... The great wonder is that the empirical, rational journey of science should have any contact at all with spiritual traditions. But in our century, the mechanistic period of science opened out to include a science of mystery ... the dawning recognition that the universe and Earth can be considered as living entities; the awareness that the human person, rather than being just a separate unity within the world, is the culminating presence of a billion-year process; and the realisation that, rather than having a universe filled with things, we are enveloped by a universe that is a single energetic event, a whole, a unified, multiform and glorious outpouring of being'.[79]

We are filled with wonder when we contemplate these words of our Pope to us: 'The universe with all its multiple, manifold relationships shows forth the inexhaustible richness of God'. We all come from the same first Flaring Forth. So, are we really the stuff of stars?

'A star could not, by itself, become aware of its own beauty or sacrifice. But the star can, through us, reflect back on itself. In a sense, you are the star. Every element was forged in temperatures a million times hotter than molten rock, each atom fashioned in the blazing heat of the star. Your eyes, your brain, your bones – all of you is composed of the star's creations. You *are* that star, brought into a form of life that enables life to reflect back on itself. So, yes: the star *does* know of its great work, of its surrender to allurement, of its stupendous contribution to life, but only through its further articulation – YOU ... When we deepen our awareness of the simple truth that we are through the creativity of stars, we begin to feel fresh gratitude. When we reflect on the labour required for our life, reverence naturally wells up within us. Then, in the deepest regions of our hearts we begin to embrace our own creativity. What we bestow on the world allows others to live in joy. Such a stupendous mystery!'[80]

# 18

## THE BREATH, THE HEARTBEAT – THE TOUCH OF THE HOLY SPIRIT

*'Nature as a whole not only manifests God but is also a locus of his presence. The Spirit of life dwells in every living creature and calls us to enter into relationship with him.' (National Conference of the Bishops of Brazil). Discovering this presence leads us to cultivate the 'ecological virtues'. [LS 88]*

'Nature as a whole not only manifests God but is also a locus of his presence.' This is a startlingly simple, yet profound statement from the bishops of Brazil. 'The Spirit of life (notice their deeper and wider image of God) dwells in every living creature (Creation and Incarnation) and calls us into a relationship with (*and experience of*) the divine' (italics mine). If we are ever going to access something of the mystery we are looking at here, then we need a more profound way of thinking and of seeing which necessitates our making time for the regular practice of meditation. This discipline will lead to an awareness that can only emerge from the deepest places within us, belonging to the very beginnings and consequent evolution of our being. To be sure, this transforming awareness is accessible to all of us – but it takes determination, discipline, patience and perseverance.

Pope Francis is also pointing out here that it is the Holy Spirit ('the Spirit of life'), the living energy of all things, that weaves the trillions of relationships throughout all of nature. So often the work of the Holy Spirit is abysmally misunderstood. Karl Rahner deplores the poverty of our theology of the Spirit, believing that it fails to recognise the Spirit's universal role, significance and primal potency in generating the process of evolution leading to the eventual completion of Creation. He anticipates the Pope's comments about the work of the Spirit, revealing the divine power in the deepest heart of each person, and of this earthly world. This power is the graced centre of Creation, divinely imbued with the evolving potential to reach its completion when God will be 'all in all'. Rahner writes, 'And here the earth behind her continual development in space and time, sinks her roots into the power of the all-mighty God ... his Spirit has already begun to transform the world into himself ... and the new Creation has already started, the new power of a transfigured earth is already being formed from the world's innermost heart.'[81]

Pope Francis wants us to grasp the closeness, the unity, the intimacy between the Spirit and all Creation. They are inseparable. This is an astonishing realisation for us, and we have to truly make it our own in mind and heart if it is ever going to lead us towards the 'ecological virtues' and spiritual conversion he pleads for. Teilhard de Chardin had a unique insight into the interweaving of the evolving planet and the work and play of the Holy Spirit. His Pentecost moment came when he was inspired to recognise that all becoming and developing in an expanding universe is animated by the divine drive of the Holy Spirit. 'For Teilhard,' wrote Ursula King, 'the heart of God is found at the heart of the world, and the living, natural world is shot through with the presence of the divine, with what he eventually was to call "the divine milieu".'[82]

Diarmuid O'Murchu's In the Beginning was the Spirit liberates the Holy Spirit from our deadly doctrinal descriptions and definitions. 'Spirit,' he writes, 'is the wellspring of all possibility, the restless pulsation of every movement of Creation and of every desire in the human heart. It is the power of becoming that awakens every stir of imagination, wisdom, creativity ... We strive for something more because deep within us, the Spirit lures us to do so.' The restlessness is a divine one, the fruit of the enlivening, energising, empowering and uniting Spirit that blows where it will, and that never ceases to amaze and surprise us. This is the 'spirit of life' that Pope Francis wishes to reveal to us during these pivotal times in the journey of the Church. At such times, O'Murchu believes that 'we know instinctively and intuitively that all is one, that relationship defines the very core of life itself.'[83]

Our lives, our faith, our prayer, our grasp of the significance of evolution are all radically transformed when we see them through this understanding of the Holy Spirit, through this lens of Incarnation. Does this dawning realisation lead to falling on our knees in personal and universal contemplation and adoration? Of course it does. All the writers we are quoting in this book give examples of this breakthrough. De Chardin, for instance, prayed: 'I love you for the extensions to your body and soul in the farthest corners of Creation through grace, through life, through matter. Lord Jesus, you who are as gentle as the human heart, as fiery as the forces of nature, as intimate as life itself, you in whom I can melt away and with whom I must have mastery and freedom; I love you as the world, as this world which has captivated my heart; and it is you, I now realise, that people, even those who not believe, sense and see through the magic immensities of the cosmos.'[84]

Pope Francis is telling us that this 'Spirit of life' lives in the core of the natural universe, firing and energising its inevitable evolution, tenderly 'calling us to enter into relationship' with him, holding all creatures in their finitude and death, and urging and drawing the world forward towards an unfathomable future. Beautiful, comforting, healing words for millions of us.

## A FURTHER WORD

*The much-neglected Holy Spirit, the Spirit of Life, the Energy of Love, is at the core of all we are discussing – the Holy Spirit who dwells outside organised religion as well as within it. This Holy Spirit of evolution belongs to all Creation and not to any one particular religious institution. And the New Universe Story of Creation prompts us to place the Holy Spirit ahead of us; not pushing us from the back only, but alluring us forward into the beating heart of the beautiful mystery.*

'Christian theology and popular devotion have both colluded in keeping the erotic Spirit tamed, and keeping its enthusiasm sheltered in an ecclesiastic enclave, seeking to protect its divinity to justify power and its holiness, to justify escape from our sinful world. The Spirit, however, belongs primarily to our world and not to any church or religion. In the indigenous tradition of the Great Spirit, the Spirit imbues creation in each and every vibration of its evolutionary unfolding. The Spirit has fared better in creation than in the Church.'[85]

'For Professor John Haught, evolution is not just driven from the past but also empowered by the lure of the future. Here we glimpse the Spirit at its most inventive and innovative. I suspect in fact that the lure of the future is far more significant than the drive from the past. The Spirit that blows where it wills is the surprising catalyst, forever breaking open novelty and extravagance – and not merely in the foreseeable future, but far beyond our conventional notion of timespace, as cosmologists press forward into new visionary horizons of an open universe without beginning or end ...

'The future attracts and invites us to move forward, informing every aspect of our being and becoming. We strive for something more because deep in our hearts the Spirit lures us to do so. The restlessness within us is a divine one, the fruit of the enlivening, energising and empowering Spirit, the same Spirit that blows where it wills and never ceases to amaze and surprise us. At all times, the Spirit is always several steps ahead of us'.[86]

# 19

## TREAD ON A DAISY AND TROUBLE A STAR

*As part of the universe, called into one being by the Father, all of us are linked by unseen bonds and together form a kind of universal family, a sublime communion which fills us with a sacred, affectionate and humble respect. 'God has joined us so closely to the world around us that we can feel the desertification of soil almost as a physical ailment, and the extinction of a species as a painful disfigurement' ... Everything is connected. Concern for the environment thus needs to be joined to a sincere love of our fellow human beings and unwavering commitment to resolving the problems of society ... We have only one heart ... [LS 89, 91, 92]*

The Pope here emphasises the intense inter-relatedness, interconnection, mutuality and oneness of all Creation. When one element of Creation is damaged or destroyed, all suffer – especially, he insists, the poor and the weakest of all creatures in the one chain of being. Humans carry an intrinsic responsibility for the well-being of our planet. In what way? We are the consciousness of the Earth. The Earth is our body. We are its head and heart. Human beings reflect back to nature her loveliness, to all non-human creatures their diversity and beauty. When our planet suffers, we suffer. This should be obvious enough. The Earth is our Mother. When she is diminished we are all diminished. The Pope expresses this truth so graphically. 'We have only one heart,' he writes, 'and the same wretchedness which leads us to mistreat an animal will not be long in showing itself in our relationships with other people. Everything is related, woven together by love.' When anything dies, a piece of each one of us does too.

John Donne captures the interwoven wholeness and dissolution across all Creation:

No man is an island, entire of itself.
Each is a piece of the continent, a part of the main.
If a clod be washed away by the sea
Europe is the less.
... Each man's death diminishes me.
Therefore, send not to know
For whom the bells tolls.
It tolls for thee.[87]


'Everything is connected,' the Pope wrote. There is no longer a dualistic separation between any aspects of God's Creation, or between Creation and God. Yet Catholicism is divided on this issue. We, ordinary mystics, believe the Pope with full hearts; yet many elements in the Roman Catholic Institution resist his 'catholic imagination'. This is worrying. The beautiful mystery of the Incarnation remains unexplored in depth. So many fail to understand that God is the Author, Creator, Mother of all that exists, the Great Designer and Artistic Imagination of the process of evolution. God's fire already burns in the darkest depths of the living earth. Ultimately, for the Christian, the Holy Spirit is present as the innermost mystery of all things, and may be understood as the invisible power at work in a continually evolving universe until God be 'all in all'. There is now no longer a destructive dualism between the things of God and the things of Earth. Karl Rahner reminds us that when we want both the God of infinity, and the spirit within our familiar, evolving universe, there is one path to both. 'Everything,' he wrote, 'is connected.'

The mystics know this. The mystic in all of us knows it. The fundamental interconnectedness and perennial allure of all things for each other belongs to the exciting realms of deep mystery and the mystical vision. Fritjof Capra, a Creation-centred physicist, believes that the '[T]he universe is seen as a dynamic web of interrelated events'.[88]

And Meister Eckhart reminds us that 'Everything in the heavens, on the earth and under the earth, is penetrated with connectedness, penetrated with relatedness.' It is for all of us, each moved by the desire to know more about this astonishing revelation, to find the books, the people, the places, the courses that will deepen our knowledge and satisfy our hunger for the wisdom so long denied us.

A favourite word of Pope Francis in his encyclical is 'compassion'. He believes that a deep communion with nature and our fellow human beings cannot be real without a sense of compassion. In this extract he tries to convince us that it is only from this sense of a shared identity that our love and care and compassion for the planet arises. It is from this sense of one-ness, of connectedness, of being a part of everything that human compassion springs: through 'long looking' (Thoreau) we sense an affinity with flora and fauna, with earth, sky and sea, with all creatures. Everything is sustained in life by the incarnate energy of our Mother-God. Unknowingly, we are all held together, all energised, all supported by the invisible bonds of relationship and love. 'When we try to pick out anything by itself,' wrote Scottish-born American naturalist John Muir, 'we find it hitched to everything else in the universe.'

On the day he died, monk and mystic Thomas Merton said, 'The whole idea of compassion is based on a keen awareness of the interdependence of all these living beings, which are part of one another, and all involved with one another.' Love's heart cannot be compartmentalised. Pope Francis reminds us that 'When our hearts are authentically open to universal communion, this sense of fraternity excludes nothing and no one.' Love makes us sensitive to any pain in any part of God's creation.

## A FURTHER WORD

*Teilhard de Chardin describes this oneness, this connectedness, this interdependence, this compassion as 'living in the divine milieu'. By this he means having our presence, our being in the very atmosphere, surroundings and environment of God – where our own lives and God's are intimately indistinguishable.*

'Teilhard's ardent spirituality was nourished by his Christian faith, but also deeply embedded in a unifying worldview, a unique synthesis which brought together elements of science, philosophy, religion, and spirituality. He always looked for a pattern in the development of things and asked above all about the significance of the human being in the vast universe. His search for overall oneness, for the unification of all things, made him see the unity of matter and spirit. Thus the universal stream of becoming, which is evolution, was understood as a process of progressive spiritualization through increasing union ...

'... The divine presence in the world is this mysterious "milieu" radiating throughout all levels of the universe, through matter, life, and human experience. We are immersed in this milieu, we are bathed in it. It can invade our whole being and transform us, if we but let it. Teilhard called it also a "mystical milieu," a "divine ocean" in which our soul may be swept away and divinized. All realities, all experiences, all our activities, all our joys and suffering, have this potential for divinization, for being set on fire through the outpouring of divine love.'[89]

Pope Francis wants us to be at home in our world, citizens of planet Earth' ... joined to the universe ... one heart beating in all dimensions of creation ... everything is connected in a universal ... we are all one.' As we have seen, we have two basic stories here – the story of Creation and the story of Incarnation. They both spring from love, the Christian believes; they are sustained by love, they will one day be completed by love. And that loving completion will happen in your own deepest being. Why? Because you are the Universe Story; you are the Christian story. Judy Cannato helps us to understand this:

'The Universe Story and the Christian story resonate together. Each uses different language, but both point to a single reality – that there is the one creation from which all life comes ... Each provides a different lens for interpreting reality itself. Each is a story of universal connectedness. Each invites us out of a narrowly focused view of the world and into a place of awe and wonder, and each resonates with a field of an emerging consciousness that invites us to engage our self-reflective awareness, our quests for knowing, our love and our freedom on behalf of all life ... While the New Universe Story flows from science, and the Christian story from religious tradition, each is rooted in, and attends to the dynamic and creative impulse at the heart of the cosmos. We can use different words; yet at the core we are speaking of the single reality that is at our own core. We are the Universe Story. We are the Christian story. Language may vary but the message is the same; we're here as a result of a single, radically amazing evolutionary process over billions of years of grace.'[90]

# 20

## THE DIVINE ARTIST AND HUMAN LOVER WHO REVEALED OUR MYSTERY TO US

*The Lord invited others to be attentive to the beauty that there is in the world, because he himself was in constant touch with nature, lending it an attention full of fondness and wonder. As he made his way throughout the land, he often stopped to contemplate the beauty sown by his Father and invited his disciples to perceive a divine message in things ... [LS 97]*

These are wonderful and revealing words by our Pope. They provide us with a picture of Jesus sauntering along the morning roads of Palestine, attentive to everything going on around him, greeting the people, listening to the birds, watching the clouds, pausing by a river, asking questions, touching a leaf and in doing so praising his beloved Father. These words and images are the heartbeat of Incarnation – the very love and meaning at the Christian core. There is a pure beauty folded into the features of our world, a divine presence in every presence, God's burning heart warming every human heart. Far from being the place of our exile, this Earth is God's home and therefore ours. The Pope calls us to renew our minds in Christ. And our theology too. There is a new story, a rediscovered understanding of who we are, of Creation, evolution, Incarnation, of God. An astonishing love story is being revealed. Blessed are they who can perceive eternity in every passing minute, who can experience something of God in every vicissitude of life.

The Pope is telling us about a new way of looking, a new way of seeing, a new way of being. This is what Incarnation has revealed – 'Behold; I make all things new!' Jesus asked us to 'Lift up your eyes and see the fields ...' (Jn 4: 35). Many people are learning how to sit and gaze at the scene before them – the rivers and hills, the soil they walk on and the heavens above them, the weeds at their feet and the distant horizon, the setting sun and the rising moon, winter's withering and spring's awakening, the rainbow's arch of peace over the frantic morning rush hour, the starry sky over silent city streets. Their attentive gaze is full of 'fondness and wonder'. They look at, then they see, recognise, experience and adore these ordinary epiphanies of divinity.

The Pope is asking us to notice the 'divine message in everything'; to ask ourselves what lies hidden in these daily sights and sounds. What might these moments have to say to you at the deepest levels about your struggles with your life just now, about the quality of your relationships and emotions, about how you see God, about your restlessness, your courage, your pain, your hopes? Jesus asks us to look again at the sparrows, the lilies, the fields. The seeds of beauty are scattered everywhere. But we have to be aware, alert, alive, to be open, to be willing, to be ready. The kingdom of God is like a grain of mustard seed, like yeast in the flour, like treasure hidden in the field, like a merchant in search of fine pearls, like a dragnet cast into the sea (Mt 13: 31). Real beauty is not showy. Only those with eyes to see will pause long enough to be astonished.

Fyodor Dostoevsky believes that 'only beauty will save the world'. Philosopher John Macmurray, as he considers today's world, writes in *Freedom in the Modern World*: 'For human life, beauty is as important as truth; beauty in life is the product of real feeling. The strongest condemnation of modern industrial life is not that it is cruel, materialistic, wearisome and false but simply that it is ugly and has no sense of beauty ... If we want to make the world better, the main thing we have to do is make it more beautiful. We have to recapture the sense of beauty if we are not to lose our freedom. There are signs, small signs – of a revival in, and reverence for beauty amongst us'.[91] The true beauty of the world is the radiance of divinity shimmering through all realities perceived by our senses. According to Gerard Manley Hopkins ' ... it will flame out like shook foil ...'. Our evolving planet Earth has always been the first sacrament of God's beauty.

There is a sacramental moment I remember well. It was a dark, eerie Friday afternoon at the end of March 1970, outside our parish nursery school overlooking the (then) foggy, murky city of Sheffield. The children were streaming to freedom towards the waiting bus. Suddenly a small girl noticed the magnificent rainbow. There it was, a bow of beauty, elegant as a leaping ballet dancer, stretching gracefully across the bloodshot sky of our industrial city. Her companions gathered around her. Fine-tuned as they were to the play of light and shade, to the dance of colours from their Lenten class preparation for the imminent celebration of the Feast of Brightness, their young eyes missed nothing in that curved miracle of wonder that hung like a silent crescent of blessing over their homes and hearts, almost within reach of their small hands. Their teacher quietly joined them. Would she talk about God, about Easter, about giving thanks? She didn't. The still wonder of the children, their awed silence, this timeless moment was pure worship. In *Art and the Beauty of God – A Christian Understanding*, Bishop Richard Harries wrote, 'There need be no question of thanks or praise as a separate event, something done afterwards. To experience the tiny theophany is itself to adore'. As the Pope indicated, true beauty needs no explaining.[92]

## A FURTHER WORD

> *In many of these extracts Pope Francis is inviting us to transform our images of God. He has an affinity with the notion of 'magnanimity' and 'imagination'. The Christian God is the creative Mother of everything that lives. How big, how utterly free do we allow that God to be?*

'God appears as an artist whose concerns transcend the values of economy and pragmatism and whose signature is a beauty that is both tender and awesome. God the Creator is the divine artist who brings forth a world that is fit to open the human spirit to beauty, goodness and love – in short, to values that move beyond everyday usefulness. And for the eye of faith, the world which God is now fashioning is truly a window to the divine. The cosmos as seen through the lens of modern science need not be a threat to belief in God. But such a vision of the world, does, indeed, confront us with a question of great importance: How big a God do we believe in? It certainly gives reason to reflect on the creative artistry of the Creator.'[93]

This 'big' God wants us to be big also. It is why Incarnation happened – so that we could realise the size of our souls, the artistry of our being. It is a huge breakthrough for us when we begin to realise that what empowers us, breaks open for us the presence of God in the most ordinary events and experiences, is a truly sacramental moment. Jesus' intense presence to nature in the fields of his mission was an act of worship before the creative imagination of his Father. And the artists around us play a central part in removing the veil that conceals the incarnate light 'in the beauty around us'. They hold the key to unlocking the corridors of connection between the 'inscape', the 'interiority', the inner core of things – and the experience of God's own self. (*LS* 97)

In his *Letter to Artists* (1999) Pope John Paul II wrote, 'None can sense more deeply than you artists, ingenious creators of beauty that you are, something of the pathos with which God at the dawn of creation looked upon the work of his hands. A glimmer of that feeling has shone so often in your eyes when – like the artists of every age – captivated by the hidden power of sounds and words, colours and shapes, you have admired the work of your inspiration, sensing in it some echo of the mystery of creation with which God, the sole creator of all things, has wished to associate you ... With loving regard, the divine Artist passes on to the human artist a spark of his own surpassing wisdom, calling him to share in his creative power.' The Pope went on to emphasise that 'Every genuine art form in its way – from writers, painters, sculptors, poets, film-makers, playwrights, composers, architects, musicians, actors – is a path to the inmost reality of man and of the world ... That is why [the Incarnation] of truth was bound from the beginning to stir the interest of artists, who by their very nature are alert to every epiphany of the inner beauty of things.' Each work of art, he said, 'which explores the everyday, the darkest depth of the soul', is 'an appeal to mystery', a 'genuine source of theology', a 'moment of grace', 'a kind of sacrament making present the Incarnation in one or other of its aspects.'

# 21

## EVERYTHING IS BEAUTIFUL IN ITS OWN WAY

*Jesus was far removed from attitudes which despised the body, matter and the things of the world ... Unhealthy dualisms left a mark on certain Catholic/Christian thinkers in the course of history, and disfigured the Gospel. Jesus worked with his hands in daily contact with the matter provided by God to which he gave form by his craftsmanship. [LS 98]*

With customary accuracy Pope Francis pinpoints the wound in the Church that perennially drains its life blood. 'Dualism' is the plague that has blighted the growth of the Christian community from the very beginning, the huge virus that has deeply infected the vitality of divine revelation, the flawed compass that is still pointing in the wrong direction. It utterly skews the meaning of God's desire to become radically human. What is dualism? It is anti-Gospel; it is anti-Incarnation. It refuses to acknowledge the full fleshing of God in Jesus. It is based on a deeply flawed theology of sin and redemption, of a lost paradise, of a primal sin, that is no longer tenable in any historical sense.

Dualism denies that God willed the world as it is, or willed human beings as they are. To be finite, such a view would hold, or to be vulnerable, to fail, to die, arises from some basic human flaw biologically passed on from the 'sin of our first parents'. Therefore, dualism would insist, the true form of our humanity is set in a previous lost paradise or in a future heavenly age after this world has ended. Dualism would hold that to be human is to have gone radically astray, to be wrong-footed from the start because of what happened in the mythical Garden of Eden. It refuses to accept ignorance, mortality and mistakes as the normal condition of humanity. This deeply ingrained curse has radically ruined our beautiful story, and is, fundamentally, the main reason for the various, troubling factions in the Vatican today, as well as the serious splintering of the Catholic faith in a world hungry for healing. Bede Griffiths saw the essence of all religious progress as one from 'dualism' to 'non-dualism'.

Theologian Dorothee Sölle defines this spiritual cancer as that which sees human power and creativity as somehow detracting from God's power in our world, as though mature parents would be jealous of their children's self-esteem and self-confidence. Human creativity can never detract from the power of divine presence since their source is one and the same. Sölle senses the need to develop a theology and spirituality of Creation before it is too late. Old religious language, outdated literalism and conventional images of God and humanity must develop, for instance, from closed to open, from fear to freedom, from sin at the centre to suffering humanity at the centre, from infinite distance to a loving intimacy, from a God out there to a divine presence within. The key to the undoing of a deadly dualism is the humanity of Jesus – the non-negotiable, utter humanness of God, incarnate not just in every human heart, but in the heart of all creatures, of the whole, vast cosmos. Coming to us 'eating and drinking' (Mt 11: 19), with full emotions and close relationships, he sanctified all human experiences, revealing for us the unconditional love of God.[94]

To sum up this reflection: It is true to say that God became human so as to reveal the divine potential within all humanity and all creation. This is a far cry from the relentless emphasis on the human potential for sin, disobedience and evil, and the strange, anti-incarnational need for baptismal exorcism and the constant need to be forever making reparation and atonement for something we were never guilty of. The Incarnation tells us so much about humanity as well as about God. It is the everlasting sacrament of the possibility and capacity of each person for unity with, and for becoming like God (I Jn 3: 1–2). All of this totally orthodox theology is the necessary preamble to recovering and healing the shrinking soul of the Catholic institution. While such an empowering theology has never been in question among the saints and scholars of our centuries of debate, it is remarkable how little of it has percolated through to the homilies, the catechisms and catechesis of our day.

The Pope's main aim is to return the Church to its true doctrine – the one it has forgotten, the one that puts humanity back in the centre, that reverences 'the divinity in the tiniest speck of dust'. His understanding of Incarnation recovers the beautiful theology of Creation long lost to dualism. For too long the Church has put 'sin' in the centre – together with the escape back to heaven from this tainted world. By putting humanity and suffering back in the centre, a lot of judgemental attitudes towards homosexuality, divorce and many other issues will start to change.

The recovery and growing authority of a theology of nature and grace, and a Creation-based spirituality, now enriched by the emerging insights of the new cosmology (the study of the origins and evolution of the universe), will have profound implications for many Christian teachings, for our understanding of sacrament, for pastoral ministry, for the continuing religion/science debate and for a new evangelising of young and old. It will help, above all, to shift our self-image as fallen creatures, complicit somehow in the death of Jesus, to an awareness of our role as vital co-creators with God of a steadily developing, ever-evolving universe. We are not guilty exiles on a fallen earth – we are the beloved bearers of her divine dream.

## A FURTHER WORD

*There is no line down the middle any more between the holy and the secular, the sacred and the profane, the graced and the graceless, the saved and the unsaved, nature and the supernatural. Pope Francis clearly condemns this dualism that has infected the Church like a virus from the first centuries. A full-bodied Incarnation makes no exceptions to God's embracing of all Creation. Can you see why the subtle dualism that lives like a virus in our churches is so dangerous and destructive?*

'Dualism is to be rejected: there is no warring between soul and body as if the two were separate components, the one higher and other lower. The Incarnation teaches us that there is a wholeness to human life, which comprehends the bodily as well as the spiritual ...'. It was the French philosopher-poet Charles Péguy who exposed the self-deception of those who believe that the way to God is the way of repression of all desires for intimacy and inter-personal warmth. 'Because they love no one,' he wrote, 'they imagine they love God.'[95] Anticipating the Pope's encyclical *Laudato Si'*, theologian John F. Haught wrote, 'Dualistic deposits in Christian theology are themselves partly responsible for the feeling of cosmic homelessness that underlies our present environmental crisis. Traditionally, an exaggerated holiness, having lost its connection to the sacramental and active aspects of religion, has turned our attention towards a spiritual world existing apart from the physical universe. Today most theologians would deny that this withdrawal is consonant with the biblical vision.'[96]

In a beautiful comment Pope Francis reminds us of the importance of our 'daily contact with matter' in our understanding of Incarnation. He places the body and its senses and activities, as Pope St John Paul II and Vatican II (*Gaudium et Spes,* 22) did, at the core of our faith. Moreover, we are a primary force in the drive forward of evolution. Because of the humanity of Christ, all is grace. Nothing is 'merely' human. Our place in the grand scheme of things consists mainly of our insight regarding the extraordinary nature of the very ordinary things we do. And nobody expresses this better than Teilhard de Chardin: 'We may, perhaps, imagine that the creation was finished long ago. But that would be quite wrong. It continues still more magnificently, and at the highest levels of the world. And we serve to complete it, even by the humblest work of our hands. That is, ultimately, the meaning and value of our acts. Owing to the interrelation between matter, soul, and Christ, we bring part of the being which he desires back to God in whatever we do. With each one of our works, we labour – in individual separation, but no less really – to build the pleroma (the 'fullness'); that is to say, we bring to Christ a little fulfilment.

'God, in all that is most living and incarnate in him, is not far away from us, altogether apart from the world we see, touch, hear, smell, and taste about us. Rather he awaits us every instant in our action, in the work of the moment. There is a sense in which he is at the tip of my pen, my spade, my brush, my needle – of my heart and of my thought. By pressing the stroke, the line, or the stitch on which I am engaged to its ultimate natural finish, I shall lay hold of that last end toward which my innermost will tends.'[97]

# 22

## GOD COMES TO US DISGUISED AS ORDINARY, AS PAIN, AS 'WHAT HAPPENS'

*From the beginning of the world, but particularly through the Incarnation, the mystery of Christ is at work in a hidden manner in the natural world as a whole, without thereby impinging on its autonomy. The creatures of this world no longer appear to us merely under their natural guise because the risen One is mysteriously holding them to himself and directing them towards fullness as their end. The very flowers of the field and the birds, which human eyes contemplated and admired, are now imbued with his radiant presence.* [LS 99, 100]

Again, this is such beautiful language of disclosure, of revealed depth, of Incarnation. The Pope's magnificent words unlock our neglected imagination and open the eyes of our souls to the treasure house of surprises lavished on us by the Divine Heart of Life. The invisible God is now visible in every step of our every journey, every day of our lives. Revelation is about how to see everything in a delightfully renewed way, using the most divine gift of God's imagination now incarnate in all of us. According to Victorian poet Christina Rosetti it is grace that teaches our hearts to see and to recognise.

> Lord, purge our eyes to see
> Within the seed a tree,
> Within the glowing egg a bird,
> Within the shroud a butterfly.
> Till taught by such, we see
> Beyond all creatures Thee.[98]

Theologian Noel Dermot O'Donoghue, in *The Mountain behind the Mountain,* writes of a Celtic and Catholic sensitivity to the reality of this invisible 'radiant presence' referred to by the Pope. This graced sensitivity to the invisible shimmering of divine beauty in 'the very flowers and birds' of nature is another papal reference to the Catholic mystical belief in the 'sacramental imagination' when the invisible world of a divine presence breaks through into our tangible and visible world of the senses and daily experiences. 'The angelic world opens up at the margins of this world where a kind of imagination reveals tentatively and faintly, never obviously, a world of light so delicate and tenuous that it is blown away by religious dogmatism and scepticism.'[99] The expression of this most special awareness of, sensitivity to, and glimpse of what the Pope is trying to convey to us, most often needs new words. Beautiful words transform the soul, they warm the heart, they set the imagination on fire. We live and move and have our being when we carry beautiful words inside us. The Pope knows this. That is why he reaches for his own inner poet, and relies on the artistic expressions and gifts of others.

Poets of nature such as William Wordsworth and Gerard Manley Hopkins know that the hidden beauty they sense (what we would call the 'catholic vision' of Incarnation) must first be experienced in their own hearts before they attempt to shape and open it up for others. Wordsworth looks behind the phenomena or 'appearances' of nature, and discovers within himself 'a sense of something deeply interfused', which has its dwelling 'in the light of setting suns and the round ocean and the living air'. Hopkins celebrates the unique 'inscape' of 'dappled things' (including 'a brinded cow') and delightedly weaves magic around the subtle light that emanates from the invisible presence within them. He writes of that 'dearest freshness deep down things' that he touches in everything, everywhere. Nor is it always about things bright and beautiful. The imaginative revelation within Incarnation must always be true to the vicissitudes and realities of life. T. S. Eliot, for instance, finds in an urban wilderness the presence of 'an infinitely gentle, infinitely suffering thing'. Mary Oliver finds heaven in 'a few weeds in a vacant lot'. Patrick Kavanagh sees 'that beautiful, beautiful, beautiful God' taking fleshy shape and 'breathing his love by a cutaway bog' in Ireland.

The Pope cherishes the notion of 'presence' – that divine indwelling within creation and humanity – to convey a glimpse of his understanding of the implications of Incarnation. Noel Dermot O'Donoghue quotes from 'The Wilderness' by Kathleen Raine, the wonderful poet of Celtic tradition – about an abiding, unending presence:

> I came too late to the hills. They were swept bare
> Winters before I was born of song and story ...
> A child I ran in the wind on a withered moor
> Crying out after those great presences who were not there,
> Long lost in the forgetfulness of the forgotten ...
> Yet I have glimpsed the bright mountain behind the mountain,
> Knowledge under the leaves, tasted the bitter berries red,
> Drunk cold water and clear from an inexhaustible fountain.[100]

Another reminder that artists and mystics (like ourselves) believe there are three ways of perceiving something. First, we may simply *look at* things quickly for information: Is it raining outside? Second, people may look at something so as to *see* it deeply, to be drawn into it, to delight in it, and then they may want to paint it, photograph it, write a poem about it, move beyond first appearances. And, finally, the observer may take a further step into what is before her, what is happening around her, and begin to *recognise* a sublime Presence in what is being observed. This is often described as an *epiphany* (a revelation of God), a sacramental moment of recognition for the true Christian, a glimpse of divine light coming through the familiar. The observer is no longer an observer; her presence now shines with the light itself.

## A FURTHER WORD

*There are no limits to the implications and experiences of Incarnation. For the friend who sent in the following account, the incarnate God was local and personal.*

'It was dark and I was taking the washing off the line. The lights streamed into the darkness from the kitchen where my three girls were sitting around the table, cups of tea in hand, chatting about their day. Through the window I watched the interaction between them, saw their animated faces, and suddenly knew that right there, in the heart of my own home, God's beauty-filled Spirit was present. A beautiful presence that set the place into radiance.' Paula had first *looked* casually at her surroundings as she re-entered her home. Then she had paused to *see* more deeply into its framed beauty. And then, remembering the meaning of Incarnation, she had *recognised* the divine presence in that moment of epiphany.

For Teilhard de Chardin the human and divine Risen Christ is also cosmic. He was the centre of the scientist's heart and the centre of the universe.

Ursula King points us towards the faith of de Chardin, which 'was thoroughly incarnational and thoroughly Christocentric. He attached a realism to the doctrine of the incarnation which is rare. His "seeing", so often mentioned in his writings, was rooted in the experience of the senses, in touching and tasting, which nourished his inner perception of the spiritual essence of things. For him, Christians need to be animated and fired by a "cosmic consciousness" which meets God through the abundant, beautiful, and awesome realities of the earth, even though God is also distinct from creation. For Teilhard, the figure of Jesus Christ is not only human and divine, but also cosmic, for Christ's influence and presence can be found in all things in the world and in the cosmos.

' ... God's omnipresence in the universe is revealed to us through the incarnation, a still on-going event wherein Christ's body continues to grow of ever larger stature. The mystical, divine milieu that surrounds us, that we breathe in and can communicate with, is still expanding, intensifying, disclosing itself in the "ever-greater Christ" whose praise Teilhard's prayers put into words of surrender, prayerful union, and adoration. Our universe is a Christified universe, marked by divine omnipresence shining through both the glory and the pain of the world. Christ is the centre of the universe, he is the centre of humanity, he is the centre of every human being. Teilhard considered it his life's vocation to be at the service of this universal Christ.'[101]

# 23

## WAKE UP TO YOUR SLEEPING POWER

*We lack an awareness of our common origin, of our mutual belonging, and of a future to be shared with everyone ... Yet all is not lost ... No system can completely suppress our openness to what is good, true and beautiful, or our God-given ability to respond to his grace at work deep in our hearts. I appeal to everyone in the world not to forget our dignity ... 'As never before in history, common destiny beckons us to seek a new beginning ... Let ours be a time remembered for the awakening of a new reverence for life, the firm resolve to achieve sustainability, the quickening of the struggle for justice and peace, and the joyful celebration of life.' (*The Earth Charter*)*
*[LS 202, 205, 207]*

In a selfish society where individualism reigns, it is so easy to forget our essentially relational identity, so easy to lapse into the false isolated self as though this were the true measure of who we are. While we are most fundamentally defined by the image of the God in whom we are so carefully fashioned, we also carry the deepest attraction for everything opposed to that definition. In the world's religions and cultures there are many names for this inbuilt deviation of the human race. Catholics will be familiar with the term 'original sin', looked at elsewhere in these pages. Our lives are a continuous interaction between our true selves and our false selves, and the dividing lines are not always easy to distinguish.

'We are summoned to become fully human,' writes Bill Plotkin. 'We must mature into people who are, first and foremost, citizens of the Earth and residents of the universe, and our identity and core values must be re-cast accordingly.'[102] Many perceptive spiritual observers of human behaviour write of a gradual awakening in the human psyche.

They notice a spreading consciousness in our grasp of the flow and blockages of our evolving condition. Richard Rohr refers to a 'great turning'. It is to this emerging world view that Pope Francis is pointing. His understanding of the mystery of Incarnation inspires him to this conviction of a profound stirring within the soul of the world in these times. Yet his awareness of what he calls 'compulsive consumerism and collective selfishness' and of the litany of human deviation that punctuates his encyclical, all of which are resisting and destroying this dream of the Earth, is filling his heart with anxiety and urgency too.

The Pope calls on our inner strengths. He is a great believer in the grace at the depths of things, the resurrection that will not be thwarted, the spring in the Earth that is invincible. The pulse of grace is stronger than the destructive forces in our hearts. He writes that 'human beings, while capable of the worst, are also capable of rising above themselves, choosing again what is good, and making a new start, despite their mental and social conditioning ... embarking on new paths of authentic freedom'. Here he is calling on 'everyone' – teachers and leaders in all governmental and religious institutions of the world. He wants Catholic people of influence to be counter-cultural, the hallmark of true Christian education. His hope springs from his incarnational belief in the invincibility of the Holy Spirit.

The Pope senses that there seems to be a convergence of energy concerning a perceived and urgent realisation of a world that is rapidly destroying itself. Human beings are reaching for a more equitable and responsible society, moving towards a universal effort to make a transition to a more community-minded and Earth-aware society. '[This movement] is germinating now – in that sustainable society on which the future depends. Its seeds are sprouting in countless actions in defence of life, and in fresh perceptions of our mutual belonging in the living body of Earth – bold new perceptions deriving from both science and spirituality.'[103]

This reflection indicates the presence of two elemental forces at work – against each other. Now more aware of the devastating effects of human-made climate change on the environment, millions are beginning to seek out and practise ways of undoing the damage we notice every day, and trying to sustain and prepare the Earth for our children and grandchildren. Deeply conscious of the battle between light and darkness in an evolving world, in *Evangelii Gaudium* the Pope urges us, with hope, to be involved wholeheartedly: 'Each day in our world beauty is born anew ... Human beings arise, time after time, from situations that seemed doomed ... Resurrection is an irresistible force' (*EG* 276). He quotes from *The Earth Charter* – something not done by a Pope in an encyclical before.

Through this effort he hopes for 'the awakening of a new reverence for life – and its celebration'. 'Reverence' is such an evocative word. It is a waking up to seeing more clearly, to perceiving beauty and honouring it where we missed it before. It is a coming alive to 'presence', bringing a sense of tenderness. We desperately need to retrieve our capacity for reverence. In all of these exhortations of the Pope as reflected in the Earth Charter, the plea is that we should learn to love more, to leave behind a period of self-destruction and make a new start. This calls for a deeply personal and universal awareness about vital issues such as poverty, environmental protection, justice, peace, equality, sustainability and, eventually, a sense of celebration. But for now, changing your lifestyle, your world view, is a challenging and painful process; it is a kind of dying.

## A FURTHER WORD

*'Destiny beckons towards a new beginning.' Our Pope will not give up hope! Within everyone, he believes, is the instinct to grow, to become more, to reach maturity, to blossom, to trust their 'invincible spirit'. This spirit, this instinct, this potential, this inner energy is what Christians call the Holy Spirit.*

This is why Christians strive to become more whole and holy, to reach the stature of the True Self, what God from the beginning intended them to be. This maturing, this self-transcendence is the way of nature; it is also the way of grace. It is the presence of the holy energy of God within people, attracting them to become what they are destined for, to evolve, from the beginning, into a greater whole. It was the divine inspiration that drove both St Francis and Pope Francis to deepen their own faith and to renew the face and soul of the Church. 'As we transcend ourselves', scholar and writer Judy Cannato writes in *Field of Compassion*, 'we become more than we presently are, we become more conscious and we awaken to divine revelation, we accept God's self-communicating grace into our lives, we participate in the evolution of the cosmos ... Self-transcendence involves our capacity to grow and develop, to hold and to envision, to dream a dream and fulfil it in tangible ways.'[104] We live in a web of energies, unavoidably influenced by each other's actions, choices and decisions. 'We are all responsible to everyone for everything,' wrote Fyodor Dostoevsky. And Brian Swimme said, 'Nothing is itself without everything else'.

# 24

## 'OH, WHAT ARE YOU DOING WITH YOUR ONE WILD AND PRECIOUS LIFE?'

*Environmental education has broadened its goals ... it seeks to restore the various levels of ecological equilibrium, establishing harmony within ourselves, with others, with nature and other living creatures, with God. It should facilitate making the leap towards the transcendent which gives ecological ethics its deepest meaning. [LS 210]*

Pope Francis is forever trying to take us below the routine of things, urging us to pause and reflect on the more profound meaning of our lives. For him there is no other way to become more truly human, more 'in harmony with ourselves, with others, with nature and with God'. This depth and 'magnanimity' lie at the heart of his understanding of contemplation and education. The vision he seeks is always within rather than without. Richard Rohr puts it so wonderfully well in one of his *Daily Meditations* that we wish to repeat it: 'Material reality is the hiding place of God. It is the place of revelation. But we must go deep to see that. What makes a thing sacred or profane is precisely whether we live on the surface of things or not. Everything is profane if you live on the surface of it; everything is sacred if you go to the depths of it, even your sin. So, the division for the mystic, is not between sacred and secular things, but between superficial things and things at their depth – what Karl Rahner called "the mysticism of life".'

This awareness-in-depth of the current ecological crisis will persuade us to begin adopting new habits. Deep education leading to a growth in responsibility, solidarity and compassionate care is urgently needed to give ecological ethics its deepest meaning. Are we, for instance, seriously concerned about 'the common good' – or do we just pray and pay lip service to it? Are we worried about the kind of community and world that our children will inherit? What was, and is our response to the migrant/refugee crisis? What actually did we do to mitigate this global disaster? We are in an age of individualism and we are all infected; we profess to be community-minded but so often we are utterly selfish, self-protective. Pope Francis has little time for those who seek spiritual enlightenment for their own contentment and fulfilment, without any commitment to make our world a better place to live. Only a sense of a sacred universe, and the underlying connectedness of everything in it, will sensitise our conscience to the hidden sin in many of our careless lifestyles, and to the selfishness in much of our prayer life.

We have not been helped in the past to be sensitive to these pressing issues about our destruction of the Earth and the terrible consequences, especially for the people and places of poverty. The world was not created for our wilful exploitation of it. Lord Rees, astronomer royal, writes, 'An anthropocentric focus is too narrow; biodiversity – life – on its own has intrinsic value.' Ecologist E. O. Wilson notes, 'If our despoliation of nature causes mass extinctions, it is the action that future generations will least forgive us for.' We're mindful that we are among seven billion anxious passengers crowded on 'spaceship Earth', whose fate depends on humanity's actions during this century.

The Pope reminds us that the current global situation engenders a feeling of instability and uncertainty which becomes 'a seedbed for collective selfishness'. Self-centred and enclosed, people's greed increases. No harvest will happen in a desert. 'The emptier a person's heart is,' the Pope says, 'the more he or she needs things to buy, own, consume.' And retail therapy carries no lasting healing. This refrain, this request, these demanding reminders run, like an underground river, throughout *Laudato Si'*. 'We are always capable of going out of ourselves towards the other ... in the rejection of self-interest and self-absorption ... we need to be attuned to the moral imperative of assessing the impact of our every action and personal decision on the world around us ... If we can overcome individualism we will be able to develop a different lifestyle and bring about significant changes in society.' (208)

Pope Francis calls on our inner strengths. True to Incarnation, he is a great believer in the grace at the depth of things, the resurrection that will not be thwarted, the 'invincible spring in the depths of the earth that is invincible'. Grace is stronger than the destruction in our hearts. He writes that 'human beings, while capable of the worst, are also capable of rising above themselves, choosing again what is good, and making a new start, despite their mental and social conditioning ... embarking on new paths of authentic freedom'. The Pope clearly believes in the invincibility of the human spirit and its 'inner authority'. (*EG* 21, 26, 27) We too must believe, with God's help, in the possibility of such a transcending of our old ways: 'Behold I make all things new; I will make the rivers flow in the desert; I will put flesh on those dry bones.' During these anxious, urgent days of the Earth's illness he wants to touch something eternal in our hearts. 'In the middle of my winter,' wrote Albert Camus, 'I discovered an invincible summer'.

## A FURTHER WORD

*How do we make that 'transcendent leap into deepest meaning' suggested by the Pope? How do we work towards achieving his vision? How do we begin to nourish the old seeds of faith in us into new blossoms, to restore a lost vision of Creation, to recover a vibrant hope and expectancy regarding the emerging vision of an evolution-centred spirituality?*

Diarmuid O'Murchu offers a starting point, a heartfelt prayer, for a graced beginning. He says, 'It is time to embrace'

- the grandeur, complexity and paradox that characterise evolution at every stage, a story that continues to unfold under the mysterious wisdom of our co-creative God, whose strategies always have, and always will, outwit our human and religious desire for neat, predictable outcomes;

- that wild, erotic power for creativity, embedded in the heart of the universe from time immemorial, evoking and sustaining life in a multifarious range of possibilities, revealing a depth of wisdom and purpose that we humans have scarcely begun to acknowledge or appreciate ...
- the inspirited and relational God, who impregnates creation from the very beginning, the divine life-force we have known, loved and served long before formal religion was ever instituted, a God who reveals to us unlimited potentials for engagement, relationality and enduring hope ...
- horizons that stretch our minds and hearts to their very limits, trusting that the creative Spirit, who breaks down all boundaries and barriers, will spearhead a new relationality in which we and every other organism will rediscover its true cosmic and planetary identity ...
- the planetary and cosmic context within which our life story and the story of all life unfolds. We belong to a reality greater than ourselves, and it is within that enlarged context that we will rediscover the benign and generic mystery within which everything is endowed with purpose and meaning.'[105]

# 25

## TEACHING THE HEART TO BRING HEALING, NOT HURTING

*Only by cultivating sound virtues and habits will people be able to make a selfless ecological commitment ... All these efforts will help change the world. They benefit society, often unbeknown to us, for they call forth a goodness which, although unseen, inevitably tends to spread. Such actions can restore our sense of self-esteem, can enable us to live more fully and to feel that life on earth is worthwhile.*
[LS 211, 212]

The Pope here is continuing with his conviction that without a commitment to true education on the part of all of us, there will be no lasting conversion to an authentic care for the Earth. Only a profound dedication to the widest and deepest possible education can bring about real changes in lifestyle. Vibrant education in environmental responsibility can encourage ways of acting that directly and significantly affect the world around us. When done for the right reasons these lifestyle changes, this 'cultivation of virtues and habits', can be seen as an act of love that expresses our own dignity. Pope Francis is at pains to emphasise that only the deepest conversion in our hearts will carry any hope of making a real difference.

He is also convinced that this conversion must happen at all levels of society – from a personal transformation leading to a sharing with other agents of influence and education, right through to an advocacy with the national and international powers as they gather at international conferences across the world to face and struggle with the huge, threatening universal reality of climate change. 'A change of heart occurs,' writes E. O. Wilson, 'when people look beyond themselves to others, and then to the rest of life. It is strengthened when they also expand their view of landscape, from parish to nation and beyond, and their sweep of time from their own lifespans to multiple generations and finally to the extended history of mankind.'[106]

By holding a mirror up to politicians, charitable social groups, parish communities, seminaries and other groupings; by holding it up to ourselves and our lifestyles; by endeavouring to shape major decisions regarding international investment; by lobbying politicians; by more personal practical actions such as 'reducing water consumption, separating refuse, cooking only what can reasonably be consumed, showing care for other living beings, planting trees, saving electricity ...'; by all of these worthy and creative measures we try to influence everyone we can, and bring out the best in human beings. There is a nobility in the duty to care for creation through little daily actions, especially those that can be noticed in the most unexpected places. 'Are you polluting the world or clearing up the mess?' asks Eckhart Tolle. 'You are responsible for your inner space; nobody else is, just as you are responsible for the planet. As within, so without. If human beings clear their inner pollution, then they will also cease to create outer pollution.'[107]

> Empty Monday faces behind wet windscreens
> inching their way along the A64 into Leeds.
> The work that awaited was already destroying them.
> And then I saw him (though I had noticed him almost
>      every day).
> On the verge of the soulless carriageway his face is beautiful
>      with attention.
> His inner work completed, he is holding the details of his day
>      against an infinite horizon.
> Like a mother to her baby or a cellist to her instrument,
> like a painter to his canvas or a priest to his altar,
> the litter picker, with meticulous dedication, stoops carefully
> to renew the face of the earth.[108]

The Pope quotes Pope St John Paul II on the central role of the family regarding sowing the seeds of an early awareness: ' ... the place in which life – the gift of God – can be properly welcomed and protected ... In the face of the so-called culture of death, the family is the heart of the culture of life.' Pope Francis continues, 'In the family we first learn how to show love and respect for life; we are taught the proper use of things, order and cleanliness, respect for the local eco-system and care for all creatures. In the family we receive an integral education which enables us to grow harmoniously in personal matu-rity ... and to be grateful and to ask for forgiveness ... These simple gestures of heartfelt courtesy help us create a culture of shared life and respect for our surroundings.' (*LS* 213) They also fulfil our deep yearnings, our search for meaning.

In *Canticle to the Cosmos* Brian Swimme says that every child should be told this: 'You come out of the energy that gave birth to the universe. Its story is your story; its beginning is your beginning.' Children's hearts will recognise these wondrous words, and will soon learn to protect and to nourish the loving, evolving heart of their divine Mother Earth. And then to adore.

## A FURTHER WORD

*We are drawn and inspired from a hope-filled future rather than shackled by past failures. Christian faith is a soberly optimistic openness to the mystery lying ahead of us, and to the human capacity to meet and transform even the most dire situations. The Pope urges us 'to live more fully and to feel the worthwhileness of the abundant life on earth', and to start this new way of living now. Our stalled hearts need to be reminded of their creative, loving power.*

'Our theology of creation begins with the conviction that our very being is a pure gift from a loving, creative God. As we experience our existence within history, it is a gift laden with potential to develop ever deeper, richer realisations. Precisely what its definitive form will be like we cannot claim to know. But the Christian belief in the incarnation and resurrection of Jesus Christ challenges us to remain open to the mystery that the created universe can yet become ... Christian faith, then, is a hope-filled openness to the future. As we receive the gift of being in our birth, so we are called to receive the consummation of that gift in a future that transcends death. But the being which we receive, and the potential with which it is laden, awaken us to an active response. What we make of ourselves and of our world is crucial for the final, transforming self-gift of God by which God brings creation to its completion.'[109]

# 26

## A NEW WAY OF THINKING, OF BEING, OF SEEING

*... Our efforts at education will be inadequate and ineffectual unless we strive to promote a new way of thinking about human beings, life, society and our relationship with nature. Otherwise, the paradigm of consumerism will continue to advance, with the help of the media and highly effective workings of the market. [LS 215]*

The Pope continues to emphasise the primary place of education in enriching the minds and hearts of God's people. He sees it as the revealing threshold of a hidden goodness within Creation. He endeavours to promote all good education in its many forms as the powerful agent of transformation, the force field of Spirit-energy that stimulates and nourishes a new enlightenment. 'Deep education,' he writes, 'is happening all the time, formally and informally, in a variety of settings; at school, in families, in the media, in catechesis and elsewhere. Good education plants seeds when we are young, and these continue to bear fruit throughout life' (*LS* 209). It is a remedy and a challenge. The kernel of the work is the awakening of the person's heart and soul, of their innate imagination, of the affirming of their creativity, of their capacity for discerning the love and meaning at the heart of all creatures. The kind of education that Pope Francis writes about is a knowing in the heart, a recognising, an awakening of the divine imagination already in the young mind and psyche. (*LS* 202–221).

A teacher awakens more than she informs. She brings to consciousness what is already within and waiting. She draws out rather than crams in. She brings to birth what is already gestating; brings to bloom what is already invisibly growing. 'Speak to us of God' the cherry tree was asked, 'and the cherry tree blossomed'. Writer Leo

Tolstoy refers to this insight, 'I cannot imagine what else a teacher would do except to remind people of their capacity for the infinite'. They already know it! In 'On Knowing Something by Heart' he wrote, 'An idea becomes truly comprehensible only when we are aware of it in our souls; when it gives us the feeling that we know it already, and were simply recalling it. This was how I felt when I read the Gospels. It all seemed so familiar; it seemed that I had known it all long ago; that I had only forgotten it.'

Soul-teaching is not about external religious rites and devotions – but the conversion of the heart; it is about enabling the student to recognise fully what she already half knows, half senses, is listening out for. Why do we say that? Because it was for this moment the soul was created. Because our hearts, sacred from birth and baptism, fashioned lovingly in the divine image, somehow already sense this ever-new revelation, this astonishing love story, waiting to hear it confirmed. And then, finally, comes the midwife, *you*, to complete the divine purpose. By the divine presence in you, you open and release the divine presence in those you serve. God intended, in your birth and baptism, that you should be, in your radiant humanity, the priestesses, prophetesses, princesses and teachers of God's mercy in the classrooms of life. A few of us wrote a prayer for the mystic-teacher we all carry within us.

> Like the artist who looks at the marble and sees the hidden
>    angel,
> like the farmer who looks at his winter fields and sees the
>    waving harvest,
> like the mystic who looks at the caterpillar and sees the
>    butterfly,
> like the midwife who looks at the distressed body and sees a
>    beautiful wee baby,
> like Jesus who looked into the hearts of sinners and saw their
>    grace,
> so too do you, the teacher; you look at your students and see
>    the face of God.

> You are, thus, the revealers, the midwives of the presence of
> God already hidden in your listeners.

'By learning to see and appreciate beauty we learn to reject self-interested pragmatism.' Pope Francis wants to open our souls to the wonderfully wider spaces of God's imagination. His deep understanding of 'education' involves the whole person. Words like 'beauty', 'attraction', 'newness' and 'courage' are never far from his lips. What is required, where 'deep learning' is concerned, is a new way of being, a new way of seeing. 'If someone has not learned to stop and admire something beautiful,' the Pope says, 'we should not be surprised if they treat everything as an object to be used and abused without scruple'. If we miss the light in the things that surround us, we will miss the light in people too. 'Create a new way of thinking about human beings and their relationship with nature,' he keeps insisting. ' ... If we want to bring about deep change, we need to realise that certain mind-sets really do influence our behaviour ...[we must] promote a new way of thinking ...'. (*LS* 215)

So often, younger people grow into an ecological sensitivity, responsibility and generosity of spirit. They make significant efforts to protect the environment. Yet all around them is a world of extreme consumerism and affluence and contrary values that are almost impossible to escape. 'We are faced with an educational challenge,' the Pope repeats. This challenge is not directed only to the formal education of young and old, but to every model of education, informal and honest, home-centred and community-based, wherever people's circle of influence applies – parish meetings, liturgy preparation, *lectio divina*, Prayers of the Faithful, reading/discussion groups etc.

## A FURTHER WORD

> *Too many of our religious teachers and leaders still cling
> to medieval images of a fixed universe, a historical fall
> from an original state of innocence and an earthly life*

*of relentless atonement. It is surely time for a systematic*
*reform of theology and spirituality, with profound implica-*
*tions for our teaching, preaching and the role of Church*
*and the meaning and celebration of the sacraments.*

'Through the eyes of Teilhard de Chardin we see that the old wine-skins of Christianity can no longer hold the new wine of our time. Most of the construction and understanding of Christian doctrine happened in ages past, based on a cosmology that is no longer true. This does not mean that our theology is irrelevant; the core principles are still held to be revelatory of divine mystery. Our understanding of these core principles, however, principles of a living God, evokes new insights and dimensions consonant with our place in this expanding, radically unfinished universe.

'As far as the life of the church is concerned, its worship, sacraments and spirituality may need to undergo a refashioning that our religious ancestors could never have envisaged on the basis of their "fixist" understanding of the natural world. Fidelity to traditional theology and spirituality will, of course, be essential to the shaping of our new identity as Christians in an unfinished universe, but we shall not feel obliged to imprison our souls and aspirations in depictions of the cosmos (or the incarnation) that now seem too small for any thoughtful and educated person ... [So] our theology must think in new ways about the doctrines of God, creation, incarnation, sin, evil and redemption, grace and freedom, and the virtues of faith, hope and love.'[110]

# 27

## A PASSION FOR THE DREAM – MORE 'CAUGHT' THAN 'TAUGHT'

*A few suggestions I have about ecological spirituality. More than in ideas or concepts I am interested in how such a spirituality can motivate us to a more passionate concern for the protection of our world. A commitment this sublime cannot be sustained by doctrine alone, without a spirituality capable of inspiring us, without an 'interior impulse which encourages, motivates, nourishes and gives meaning to our individual and communal activities'. [LS 216]*

There is a mindless way of being a Catholic Christian. We carry out the required obligations regarding most doctrines and most practices of our faith and then get on with our lives as a mostly separate enterprise – except perhaps in times of need or trouble. We continually confuse the outward observance of religion with the inner transformation of the heart. We think that fulfilling Church laws is what Christianity is about. This, the Pope says, is a tragic mistake. It comes from a sin-redemption mentality, an individualistic spirituality of personal atonement, a very grim and fearful image of God. Religion all too often becomes a suffocating dead end, a stultifying straitjacket that cripples the freedom of the daughters and sons of the loving Creator.

Philosopher Martin Buber once proclaimed that 'nothing hides the face of God better than religion'! It may shock some people to hear that, and to reflect on the truth that everything in our faith – churches, sacraments, doctrines, scriptures, hierarchies – are all secondary, never ends in themselves, only pointers, facilitators, midwives to us as we try to live our lives as fully as we can. The divine wish for us is to become the people we were created to be by falling more fully in alignment with God's vision for the world, thus ushering in more swiftly the complete reign of God. That, and only that, is what gives God true worship. Pope Francis is a constant critic of any other priorities.

In this quote the Pope wants to take us beyond false ways of belonging to the Christian Church. He is well aware of the trap of the external performance rather than the inner falling in love that leads to a passionate commitment to the transformation of our hearts, to the renewal of the face of God's earth and to God's need of our cooperation. 'In the context of conversion,' writes Hugh O'Donnell in *Eucharist and the Living Earth*, 'there is a type of religious practice which merely translates the world into new ideas and paradigms, but does not go further. Conversion, in this case, stays at the level of concept; it could be caricatured as being concerned with beliefs rather than with faith.'[111] O'Donnell then refers to the wise words of the philosopher Schumacher; 'Too often we communicate at the level of the word, and we don't change the world if we leave it there; unless the word, our message, our understanding, becomes incarnate, becomes flesh and dwells among us, nothing happens. This is a very deep insight of Christianity – that unless the word comes into the material world and becomes flesh, nothing happens.'[112]

Pope Francis here mentions those Christians who misguidedly dissociate the 'life of the Spirit' from the life of the body, of nature, of the realities of the world. He is reaching beyond a habitual deference to fixed doctrinal structures, the routine repetition of rubrics and rites. Instead he calls for a wholehearted, freely chosen commitment to a more holistic and spiritual concern and love for the earth. Again, notice the strong words – 'a passion, a commitment, a nourishing and motivating inspiration'. In his earlier *Evangelii Gaudium* (2013) he revealed his main source of such a profound vision and commitment. While doctrinal pronouncements were not the basis of his faith, he had, he said, 'one dogmatic certainty – the certainty that God lives deeply in every person even if that person's life is a disaster, destroyed by vices, drugs, or anything else.'

In a brilliant sentence that captures the essence of Incarnation, that reveals his utter conviction of the raw reality of God's self-communication through an intense self-fleshing in every single aspect of Creation, we read, 'it is our humble conviction that the divine and the human meet in the slightest detail in the seamless garment of God's creation, in the least speck of dust of our planet' (9). He repeats this sacramental vision, this use of the catholic imagination, this spiritual clarity that springs from his Creation theology of nature and grace, numerous times, in beautifully lyrical language, throughout all his writings.

The Pope has never disguised his opinions about those who cannot be moved or at least be open to the present urgency of the woundedness of the Earth. He has harsh words to say, as we saw (*LS* 8), about those who damage our common home in any way – '[committing] sins against ourselves and sins against God'. Greedy and lazy (the deadly sin of sloth) they either exploit the Earth, or just cannot be bothered about taking care of her. Our mother Earth is bleeding and we are too distracted, too selfish, to give time, talent or attention to her. And only the deepest commitment will do. The Pope calls us to *become* mercy, to *incarnate* compassion in our very being. Using core, fleshy words for this – like 'visceral', 'guts' – he takes Incarnation more seriously than most Christians do. Few Christians burn with the intense cosmic and personal spirituality of the Pope.

## A FURTHER WORD

> *The heart of Pierre Teilhard de Chardin's spirituality springs from his scientific studies, interwoven with his understanding of Incarnation. The Pope clearly had 'a soft spot' for him, and we can see his influence in certain points of the encyclical (for example 83 and the footnote). We can ask ourselves if we might ever experience a moment of his utter dedication to his scientific exploration, and his whole-hearted devotion to God.*

' ... For Teilhard [de Chardin] the heart of God is found at the heart of the world, and the living, natural world is shot through with the presence of the divine, with what he eventually was to call "the divine milieu." ... More than anything else, the fire of Teilhard's words and vision may help to ignite a spark through their central spiritual insight about "living in the divine milieu" ... This is a particular way of seeing, of reflecting, and responding that holds the key to a secret that can transform every experience, every event, whether good or bad, into a significant encounter which reveals to us the breath and touch of the spirit, the ever loving heart of God. This particular way of seeing is also a spiritual discipline, a technique even, which can be learned and practiced. Its potential for transforming human life into greater growth and wholeness, into a sense of plenitude and an experience of communion, is immense. Understood in this way, the heart of Teilhard de Chardin's spirituality is truly linked to the transfiguration of ordinary life into an ardent adventure of the spirit.'[113]

# 28

## 'IN THE DESERT OF THE HEART LET THE HEALING FOUNTAINS START'

*'The external deserts in the world are growing because the internal deserts have become so vast.' (Pope Benedict) For this reason the ecological crisis is also a summons to profound interior conversion ... Living our vocation to be protectors of God's handiwork is essential to a life of grace; it is not an optional or secondary aspect of our Christian experience.*
*[LS 217]*

A regular refrain of Pope Francis, and repeated here, is the primacy of the inner life. Before setting out in pursuit of any good work, or project, or commitment, he is saying, make sure that your soul is in good shape, that your motivation is sure, that your heart is very self-aware, that you are identifying and transforming all that diminishes the guiding light within you. Before creating oases of grace for others are we first endeavouring to irrigate the 'vast deserts' within ourselves? Only love will do this. In his four major writings the Pope emphasises the unconditional nature of God's love for us. Given the flawed teaching about God's pettiness, anger and punishment by which many of us were seriously misled, he knows we find it so difficult to believe that, no matter what, we are always, already utterly loved by a God who is helplessly committed to us (hence the title of this book: *An Astonishing Secret – The Love Story of Creation and the Wonder of You*).

The Pope recounts his visit to the Contarelli Chapel in Rome to sit and contemplate Caravaggio's *The Calling of Matthew* – a profound painting that shows a group of foppish tax collectors in a sleazy-looking room, one of them leaning ever and grasping his bag of money, the centre of all their lives. What, he would ask himself, is he hiding and protecting in the unexamined depths of his soul? In his retreat notes the Pope reflects, 'What are the idols you need to strip away today, the ones that prevent you from receiving God's unconditional love? The small and great ones that block and blind your mind and soul to the divine tenderness? ... What do I hide in my heart? Is there love or hatred, forgiveness or a desire for revenge? ... what is inside will come out and do harm if it is evil, or will bless others if it is good.'

For the Pope, the authenticity of the person, the true 'who-ness' of each one is utterly central, necessary and non-negotiable. Without an awareness of the True Self all else collapses. As within, so without. Throughout *Evangelii Gaudium* he keeps identifying the precious key for deepening the ecological compassion of others as that personal experience of the Creator's love and salvation in one's own soul first. Only then will one's words carry the attractive power, conviction and personal enthusiasm to win others over. You can walk with others on this beautiful Earth only to the extent that you have walked it first within your own heart. 'Only those who themselves have *experienced* salvation can move others; and only then can they speak out their beauty,' wrote the Pope. Or, as Gandhi put it, 'Be the change you wish for others'.

This 'inner conversion' must always be happening before we can be sure-footed and confident in the vineyard where we live. We remember the words of Jesus to St Teresa, 'Without you, your abilities and your good heart, I can achieve nothing. It is through your senses that the Kingdom is built – your eyes, your ears, your touch of compassion are my Father's only way of saving the world'. The Pope writes, 'Living our vocation to be protectors of God's handiwork is central to the life of grace ...'. By virtue of our birth and baptism he is calling us to play our responsible roles as priests and priestesses of creation. Are we aware of this vocation engendered in us by virtue of our birth and baptism?

This opening extract challenges us all, and perhaps especially certain committed and prayerful Christians who tend to be dismissive of any concern for the environment, who are inclined to ridicule those who wish to clean up the Earth, and who remain passive towards and dismissive of the call to change old habits. The Pope will not have any of this reneging and denial! He insists on 'a profound interior conversion.' In *Evangelii Gaudium* he writes, 'Let us be protectors of creation, protectors of God's plan inscribed in nature, protectors of one another and of the environment' (*EG* 216). When our own hearts are empty of an active love and concern, then we will have no heart to save the world. True love is not selective; it reaches everywhere. The desert in the heart comes before the desertification of the earth. Who will provide the help we need to water those deserts? What is our Church doing to sensitise us to the urgency of the ecological challenges?

Nor can any of us take refuge in ignorance, cynicism, uncertainty, sloth, carelessness. 'Just as goodness tends to spread,' the Pope writes, 'the toleration of evil, which is injustice, tends to expand its baleful influence, and quietly to undermine any political and social system, no matter how solid it may appear' (*EG* 59). In his retreats the Pope alerts us to the way human beings contrive to feed their self-destructive vices; trying not to see them, trying not to acknowledge them. This is a new focus of attention in our 'examination of consciousness'. To stimulate passive and unconvinced Catholics, *Laudato Si'* strongly suggests an 'ecological conversion' for all of us. This demands a radical shift in our beliefs and values, a fundamental option for justice for the planet and for the most destitute of its inhabitants. And, once again, we turn to scientist and mystic Teilhard de Chardin for a glimpse of the kind of inner vision, spirituality and continual conversion that the Pope refers to as the energy for our commitment to the health of Mother Earth.

## A FURTHER WORD

*Because an ecological conversion is 'like a falling in love', it asks many questions. Are we, for instance, convinced that there is a spiritual power at work in our daily lives and in the evolution of our planet? Do we believe that here, at this stage of our evolution, is where God is most truly present? Are we really sure that the Gracious Mother-God is incarnate in all Creation, in all creatures, in all experiences? Only a wise, transformed and adoring heart could write like this:*

'Every exhalation that passes through me, envelops me, or captivates me, emanates, without any doubt, from the heart of God; like a subtle and essential energy it transmits the pulsations of God's will. Every encounter that brings me a caress, that spurs me on, that comes as a shock to me, that bruises or breaks me, is a contact with the hand of God. Every element of which I am made up is an overflow from God. When I surrender myself to the embrace of the visible and tangible universe, I am able to be in communion with the invisible that purifies, and to incorporate myself in the Spirit without blemish.

'Through him, all bodies come together, exert influence upon one another, and sustain one another in the unity of the all-embracing sphere, the confines of whose surface outrun our imagination. God is at work within life. He helps it, raises it up, gives it the impulse that drives it along, the appetite that attracts it, the growth that transforms it. I can feel God, touch him, "live" him in the deep biological current that runs through my soul and carries it with it ... The deeper I descend into myself, the more I find God at the heart of my being; the more I multiply the links that attach me to things, the more closely does he hold me – the God who pursues in me the task, as endless as the whole sum of centuries, of the incarnation of his Son.'[114]

# 29

## As within so without

*... a healthy relationship with creation is one dimension of overall personal conversion, which entails the recognition of our errors, sins, faults and failures, and leads to heartfelt repentance and desire to change ... 'To achieve such reconciliation we must examine our lives and acknowledge the ways in which we have harmed God's creation through our actions and our failure to act. We need to experience a conversion, a change of heart.' (Australian Bishops' Conference)* [LS 218]

Here Pope Francis continues his plea for putting personal and communal spirituality at the centre of everything – 'overall personal conversion', 'recognition of our errors', 'we must examine our lives and experience a conversion'. He repeats his belief that there will be no ecological conversion without a vibrant inner life. He is quite clear, as Jesus was, that only transformed hearts can transform others. (Think of his encounter with the proselytising man with the plank in his eye!) People must first experience an intimacy with God and Creation before others can *catch it off* them.

It's not only about learning lessons and doctrines; it's about catching, about deep change leading to transformation. Many find that any commitment to true spirituality, especially ecological spirituality, is missing from today's Church priorities. The interior conversion that begins with the heart must come first. That ecological conversion just *cannot* succeed without a personal conversion first. We are continually replacing this inner transformation, this enfleshing of divine love in our human hearts, with the external practices of religion. Jesus and Pope Francis have some hard things to say about hypocrites.

The Pope is insistent that we understand his distinction between 'knowledge about' and 'actual experience of'. Everything about his pontificate gives witness to that emphasis. It highlights the essential nature of the *experience* of one-ness with nature, with grace, with the depths of incarnate Love. This authentic and gradual transformation of how we see our place in an evolutionary world is bound to spur us on, and inspire us to become more responsible for, more part of everything around us in our daily living. To make us sit up and take notice the Pope talks, as we saw, about environmental ignorance and carelessness in terms of sin. A more universal 'examination of consciousness' replaces an individualistic 'examination of conscience'.

The Pope speaks of the *experience* of conversion – not just good resolutions and sporadic forays into concern for the world – but a lasting experience that becomes an inherent part of our deepest soul, part of our passion and devotion to our Mother Earth. This urgent and personal theme of a transformed consciousness continues throughout his writings. The Pope pleads here for a change of our hearts, of our outlook, of a sense of our conscientiousness and dependability for the whole world. Are we, for instance, colluding with the deadly threat and destruction caused by climate change, contributing to its increasingly harmful effects by our ignorance of it, our denial of it, asks the Pope? Have we a heartfelt repentance for the carelessness of our lives in the past, our failures and sins where a real love of our Mother Earth is concerned?

We resent so many of these impositions. They challenge our comfortable habits and our habitual comforts. Lord Deben, Chair of the UK Independent Committee on Climate Change, writes, 'Yet the truth is bleak and stark and there is a moral requirement to accept and act on that truth. Those who rape the earth and destroy the climate's equilibrium also destroy the human soul, especially the lives and loves of the poor of the earth. We were not made for this, and we have it in our power to change – ourselves and our world.' Pope Francis agrees. 'For all our limitations, gestures of generosity, solidarity and care cannot but well up within us, since we were made for love ... [God's voice] is not the voice of a commentator but of an anxious father who is trying to heal the deepest concerns of his children.' The Father's anxiety is about the broken relationship between human beings and their environment. The Buddhists teach about 'right relations'. You will find this deepest concern at the heart of all great religions, inscribed into the beliefs of the earliest cultures and civilisations.

The Australian Bishops' Conference suggests that any relevant reconciliation will only emerge from the efforts to find the causes of our blindness and isolation. Many would hold that some kind of fear is ingrained in all human resistance to creating new unities and communities, new forms and formations. What kind of fear? Fear of losing control, fear of losing power, fear of losing independence and autonomy. A great love is needed. There has to be the 'magnanimity', the abundance of which the Pope so frequently writes, a bigness of vision, a huge generosity of heart, without which our convictions and good intentions will wither in shallow soil. In a conversation with Richard Rohr recently about these pressing issues, Archbishop Desmond Tutu explained the South African word *ubuntu* – the essence of being human. 'Ubuntu speaks particularly about the fact that you can't exist as a human being in isolation. You cannot be human all by yourself ... We think of ourselves far too frequently as just individuals, separated from one another, whereas you are connected (with everything and everyone), and what you do affects the whole world. When you do it well, it spreads out; it is for the whole of humanity.'[115]

## A FURTHER WORD

> *It was God's intention from the beginning that Creation would evolve, in love, into Incarnation, and then, in Christ, into the final Omega of human/divine completion. How does this challenge your current understanding of God? When will the teaching Church belatedly open up to the radical changes that Vatican II tried to introduce?*

Many people, when they begin to recognise the implications of the Universe Story, ask questions like: Where is God in the new story?

Where is Jesus? Does this contradict the Christian tradition? These are significant questions that challenge us to rethink what we now believe in light of what science knows. This work will not be easy. Vatican II recognised the impact of the New Universe Story: 'And so [humankind] substitutes a dynamic and more evolutionary concept of nature for a static one, and the result is an immense series of new problems calling for a new endeavour of analysis and synthesis' (*Gaudium et Spes* 5). The Church's intellectual tradition needs to be set alight again if it is ever going to evolve along the Creator's dream for it. To respond to a world in transformation, it needs to find a new and trusting openness to change and to its divine charter, to recover its 'catholic imagination' if it is ever to discern what of its tradition is still essential, what needs to develop, and what is no longer useful. And to remember that the God of evolution is at the heart of it all.

Judy Cannato writes, 'It is clear in theologian Karl Rahner's teaching that the fact and experience of the Incarnation is not a break with evolutionary history, not an event standing outside of space-time, but a natural development in the universal bestowal of grace that leads to humankind's conscious acceptance of God's self-communication. It is essential that the Incarnation, embodied in the person of Jesus, is part of the entire experience of God's self-communication to the world'. Cannato reminds us of Karl Rahner's belief that Jesus cannot simply be God himself as *acting in* the world (a one-off intervention from outside), but must be '*part of* the cosmos, a moment intrinsically within its history, and indeed at its climax.' Jesus, then, must be 'truly [human], truly a part of the earth, truly a moment in this world's biological process of becoming, a moment in [humanity's] natural history'.[116] He is a human person 'who just like us receives in his spiritual, human, and finite subjectivity the self-communication of God in grace.'[117] Rather than a divine intervention into human history, Cannato holds, the Incarnation is the inevitable result of the evolutionary process, of matter evolving towards spirit from the very beginning.

# 30

## Your unique place in the family of Creation

*We are not disconnected from the rest of creatures but joined in a splendid universal communion. As believers we do not look at the world from without but from within, conscious of the bonds with which the Father had linked us to all beings. By developing our individual God-given capacities, an ecological conversion can inspire us to greater creativity and enthusiasm to solve the world's problems ... [LS 220]*

A mother spoke about the night she suddenly awoke and knew that her son, thousands of miles away, had died. She knew this, she said, not because of some ethereal 'message' that came to her across the world. She knew it because of the loss of a sustaining energy, a life-long life-giving spiritual connection, an invisible love between them that had suddenly snapped. Her heart woke up, not because of some new knowledge received from the outside, but because of a vital love-energy lost from deep within. 'We are joined in a splendid universal communion.' This is another wonderful papal statement. In these pages we are trying to understand it. The Pope is referring to the mystery of life and relationships and love-energy; they are like a universal web, like the veins in a leaf.

The 'ecological conversion' that Pope Francis prays for is based on this awareness, this paradigm shift in our new perspective. We become citizens of a bigger country whose boundaries are endless, stretching out to the realms of space, reaching in to the tiniest form of being living on land and in the sea. This 'becoming' evolves from within, from realising the common bond of the one universal family, the breath, energy and life common to all creation. It requires and inspires 'a spirit of generous care, full of tenderness'. This 'view from within' entails a deep sense of thanksgiving, a recognition of our responsibility for the Earth, that all is gift, inspiring us to give of ourselves in turn, in the service of our Mother-Earth and of all Creation.

How does this undercurrent of connectivity, this 'splendid universal communion' resonate with the Christian imagery of a 'Mystical Body', a 'Communion of Saints'? Can we extend and apply the same traditional notions and language at this point of partial convergence between an evolving science and an evolving theology? Is there precious, common ground in the emerging similarities currently laid open for us between the Being we call God and the Being that is Life, that is Love, that is Creation, that is 'what is', that is 'the Now' – no matter where we may find or experience these realities? The Pope asks that we immerse ourselves in the current glimpses we are given into the beautiful mysteries of Creation and Incarnation. Why? He knows they can radically enrich our faith and fundamental options regarding our prophetic role in saving the Earth.

Creation spirituality bids us pursue, in action and contemplation, these revelations about our origins, our lives, our destiny and the notion of 'oneness' that permeates everything. The fundamental interconnectedness and perennial allurement of all things for each other belong to the exciting realms of deep mystery and an emerging mysticism. Mysticism is all about shared Being, about our commonality with everything created. We are all mystics of one kind or another. Fritjof Capra is a Creation-centred physicist. 'The universe', he writes, 'is seen as a dynamic web of interrelated events'. And the 13th-century mystic Meister Eckhart points out that 'Everything that is in the heavens, on the earth, and under the earth, is penetrated with connectedness, penetrated with relatedness.'

The emergence of a living cosmology is revealing ever-new depths to the mystery of unity and intimacy in the phenomenon of universal Being. For the interested Christian this is the opening of newly discovered windows onto the wonder and artistry and sheer delightful imagination of the One we call God. As the physicists explore relentlessly into the dark secrets of space, they confess to their continual astonishment at the recurring patterns and harmonic flow that stem from, and tend toward a ubiquitous entirety; there is the reawakening of a vibrant mysticism from a long sleep, bringing home to us the interdependence of all living things that are intimately a part of one another, and inseparably involved with one another.

Mahatma Gandhi saw all life as one in a cosmic family in which each member helped to elevate the whole from a selfish, destructive level to a spiritual and productive one. And not only among the major world religions do we find insights into the mysterious oneness at the heart of everything but also among the more ancient and more heart-centred traditions of native peoples all over the world. Such Creation-centred reflections on 'oneness' are sometimes cosmological, sometimes mystical and spiritual. These disciplines are intrinsically connected. We remember Einstein's belief that 'science without religion is lame; religion without science is blind'.

There is a primordial music and dance at the heart of all created being. There is an awakening, a flowing, an allurement, a loving, a creating, a returning. 'The world is a spinning die,' according to Hasidic wisdom, 'and all things turn and spin and change, for at the root all is one, and salvation inheres in the change and return of things.'[118] Sin is when we interfere with, distort, block this rhythm, when we introduce a discordance to the evolving symphony, even to the tiniest note. There is a Pygmy legend about a forest filled with the most beautiful music. 'A little boy finds the bird with the enchanting song and brings it home. He asks his father to bring food for the bird. The father refuses to feed a mere bird. In fact he kills it. And the legend says that with the killing of the bird he kills the song, and with the song, himself. He dropped dead and stayed dead forever.'[119] Every hurt we inflict on nature leaves a scar on the Creator's face. Every time we honour the smallest creature we honour Creation, ourselves and God. Once a Zen master climbed a hill with his students to deliver a sermon. Just as he was about to open his mouth a bird sang. 'The sermon,' he said, 'has been delivered'.

## A FURTHER WORD

*Pope Francis wants us all to feel at home with this sacramental vision, this mystical awareness, this deeper insight into the secrets of the promised 'abundant life'. His wish is for us to marvel and wonder at the most beautiful images and stories that arise from a deepening understanding of this emerging world-view around the current convergence of science and religion. Our recent popes too have encouraged us all to take a deep interest in this huge challenge that will draw out of us a 'creativity and enthusiasm' (LS 30) to carry out the work of the Holy Spirit in this 'change of era'.*

'... both science and theology are bearers of important truth about the world. They answer different questions. Science is concerned with the world as a structured system operating according to natural causes. Theology is concerned with the same world as related to God. Both open different windows onto the order and beauty of the universe, its surprising fecundity, and its suffering death and finitude. Building a bridge between them can have fruitful results, despite unresolved ambiguities that may remain ... Thinking along these lines, Pope St John Paul II garnered public interest and front page headlines in 1996 in his address to the Pontifical Academy of Sciences regarding his statement that the theory of evolution is more than a hypothesis ... He declared that "new knowledge has led us to realise that the theory of evolution is no longer a hypothesis. It is indeed remarkable that this theory has been progressively accepted by researchers, following a series of discoveries in various fields of knowledge. The convergence, neither sought nor fabricated, of the results of work that was conducted independently, is in itself a significant argument in favour of this theory".'[120]

# 31

## IT IS THE SAME LIGHT – IN THE BIG BANG, IN THE BETHLEHEM STAR, IN THE MASS CANDLE, IN THE HUMAN HEART

*Each creature reflects something of God, and has a message to convey to us – the knowledge that Christ has taken unto himself this material world and now, risen, is intimately present to each being, surrounding it with his affection, filling it with his light ... Then, too, there is the recognition that God created the world, writing into it an order and a dynamism that human beings must embrace. [LS 221]*

Here is another powerful passage, utterly incarnational and sacramental. This is God's own incarnate body we're talking about! Have we the imagination, the eyes of faith to see it that way? And to see everything that way too? The challenge for the Christian is to sense that God is always incarnate, always present, hiding just below the surface of our daily lives. Every moment of authentic experience carries the felt message for us of divine grace. God is the energy that sustains all our human happenings and emotions. To become more aware of God's earthy, hidden dynamic all around us we need to look more intensely, listen more carefully, think more imaginatively, see more deeply, feel more attentively. Ordinary life is very sacred indeed.

This is how Irish poet Joseph Mary Plunkett puts it in 'I See His Blood upon the Rose'.

> I see his blood upon the rose
> And in the stars the glory of his eyes,
> His body gleams amid eternal snows,
> His tears fall from the skies.
> I see his face in every flower;

> The thunder and the singing of the birds
> Are but his voice – and carven by his power
> Rocks are his written words ...[121]

Finally comes the poet! Pope Francis is well aware of the inability of a cerebral approach to move the heart. He calls up the services of the senses. Through music, poetry, painting and film he appeals to our deeper selves. Traditionally western Christian theology has been predominantly concerned with the understanding of God through conceptual and rational concerns. While rational thought and concepts are vital in our attempts to come to an understanding of God, a purely verbally based theology is an impoverished one. Way back in the 19th century, Matthew Arnold was suggesting that poetry is a key component in establishing harmony between science and religion. 'More and more,' he wrote, 'humanity will discover that we have to turn to poetry to interpret life for us, to console us, to sustain us. Without poetry our science will appear incomplete; and most of what now passes for religion and philosophy will be replaced by poetry'.

Pope Francis is well aware that without his skilful grasp and delight in bringing works of art into his current mission, it will fail. A genuine work of art has the power to evoke in people emotions of awareness, of wonder, of belonging, stirring the deeper longings of the soul for a sublime intimacy. He is trying to get us to fall in love with our world so as to nourish our desire to save it from all that is seriously threatening it these years. From now on, our understanding of the meaning and urgent mission of Christianity today needs to be more artistic. This is not a new discovery. The Upanishads, the Bhagavad Gita and the Tao Te Ching are all poetic in nature. We enjoy the mysticism of the Sufi poets Hafiz, Rumi and Kabir, and the Buddhist poets Basho and Milarepa.

In 1983 two of our greatest mentors regarding these pressing issues –Thomas Berry and Brian Swimme – were having a meal at the Broadway Diner in New York City. Berry suddenly said, 'You scientists have this stupendous story of the universe ... But so long as you persist in understanding it solely from a quantitative mode you fail to appreciate its significance. You fail to hear its music. That's what the spiritual traditions can provide. Tell the story but tell it with a feel for its music.'[122]

## A FURTHER WORD

*This extract calls us to recognise that God 'writes into this world an order and a dynamism that human beings embrace'. But how do we do this? To help us, Teilhard de Chardin identifies the graced gift of being able to 'see', to recognise, to adore the divine presence in the only form, 'shape' and guise in which it can be perceived – the disguise of 'the ordinary'. He calls it 'the divine milieu' – living in the divine atmosphere/environment). This takes us back again to the sublime meaning of Incarnation.*

'God reveals himself everywhere, beneath our groping efforts, as a *universal milieu,* only because he is the *ultimate point* upon which all realities converge ... It follows that all created things, every one of them, cannot be looked at, in their nature and actions, without the same reality being found in their innermost being – like sunlight in the fragments of a broken mirror – at one beneath its multiplicity, unattainable beneath its proximity, and spiritual beneath its materiality. No object can influence us by its essence without our being touched by the radiance of the focus of the universe. Our minds are incapable of grasping a reality, our hearts and hands of seizing the essentially desirable in it, without our being compelled *by the very structure of things* to go back to the first source of its perfections. This focus, this source, is thus everywhere.

'Let us establish ourselves in the divine milieu. There we shall find ourselves where the soul is most deep and where matter is most dense. There we shall discover, where all its beauties flow together, the ultra-vital, the ultra-sensitive, the ultra-active point of the universe. And, at the same time, we shall feel the *plenitude* of our powers of action and adoration effortlessly ordered within our deepest selves ...'.[123]

# 32

## HAPPINESS IS HAVING ENOUGH

*Christian spirituality proposes an alternative understanding of the quality of life, and encourages a prophetic and contemplative lifestyle, one capable of deep enjoyment free of the obsession with consumption ... It is the conviction that 'less is more' ... Christian spirituality proposes a growth marked by moderation and the capacity to be happy with little. [LS 222].*

More than once the Pope speaks of the central place of 'a contemplative lifestyle' in our 'Christian spirituality'. He sees the practice of contemplation – whether in the mode of still, silent sitting, or in the context of a deeper, more mindful way of acting and contributing – as a non-negotiable basis for acquiring any real wisdom. We must have a contemplative dimension to our lives, a real surrender of our hearts to the peace, power and passion of the Gracious Mystery. It is here, during that meditative way of seeing and being, that the spiritual dimension of our lives is refined and nourished. It blesses us with the 'magnanimity' so beloved of the Pope, 'expanding the horizons of our hearts and minds' in our praying and presence, gracing us with an ability to hold and absorb seeming contradictions, and therefore a step towards transformation. We become more loving. We see things more lovingly. Those around us become more loving.

Richard Rohr keeps pointing out that God is already here, all about us, within us and AS us – the very source, ground and fulfilment of our being. But, subject to the limitations of the human condition, we struggle to believe the truth about ourselves. That is why we meditate – that we might awaken to God's presence within us, within everything. In meditation we open ourselves to the realisation that our very being, and the being of everyone and everything IS the way God lives in our world. God is always loving us into being, holding us in our fragile being by every blessed breath we take, such that our very presence is the manifested presence of God. We meditate that we might awaken to this universal mystery, not just in our stillness, but in every moment of our lives. The Pope knows that this 'graced seeing' changes everything – especially the way we look at our world, making us realise why we should be trying to save it. 'We are created,' wrote St John Chrysostom, 'to be manifestations of God's beauty'. There is no other way for God to be present, to be known to be loved. Only through Creation. 'If humankind could have known God without the world, God would not have created the world,' said Meister Eckhart in the 13th century.[124]

When we see our planet as beautiful, beloved and broken, when we catch glimpses of our Earth-Mother and Earth-family struggling desperately in their sublime but seriously damaged bodies, a whole new tenderness and compassion fills our hearts, urging us to listen to the Pope and to do what he is begging us to do. And little by little we come to that point of blessedness and freedom and insight in which we can say, along with St Paul, 'For me to live is Christ' (Phil 1: 21). That means, for me to live is to experience in the midst of this world, with all its shadows and lights, something of that unity and intimacy with our incarnate God; it means that the world is no longer just a neutral passing place on our trek to heaven, but the very home that is God's home too, constantly needing our cooperation for its recovery to a lasting health and wholeness from its current damaged beauty. 'We settle into the concrete immediacy of our breath and our bodily being. We do not fly off to another realm of being. We enter into the meaning of Incarnation; "the mind of Christ" becomes known to us in the flesh and blood of the earth, and of ourselves.'[125]

The Pope is aware of our 'obsession with consumption'. He outlines some of the practical aspects of ecological conversion, the change in our lifestyle as well-off people. He suggests taking seriously to heart 'the ancient lesson, found in the Bible and in many religious traditions, the conviction that "less is more"'. He pleads with us to discern the excessiveness in our lives today, our congenital drive towards acquiring more, often in a mindless kind of greed. Ronald Rolheiser writes that 'when excess enters, enjoyment departs, as does freedom. Compulsion sets in ... Excess is a substitute for enjoyment.' We grow by subtraction. The Pope offers practical guidelines. What do we buy? How do we vote? Do we burn coal, oil, gas? Are we working to reduce the 'ecological debt', our 'carbon footprint'?

He calls for a return to that simplicity that allows us to stop and appreciate the small things, to live in the Now, to be grateful for the opportunities that life affords us, to be spiritually detached from what we possess, and 'not to succumb to sadness for what we lack'. He is well aware of the existential power of human greed, of the drive towards a selfish acquisition and accumulation of things, of 'the dynamic of dominion' and control, of the compulsion to pleasure and the good life. He thus provides a spiritual depth and context for the often shallow values we follow. He insists on our recognition, in the prayers we say, of the intimate, beating, incarnate heart of a surrendered God at the core of Creation and of our lives.

## A FURTHER WORD

*Do you experience that presence of, and intimacy with the Creator when you pray with a full heart and act with a practical compassion? There's a real human warmth in these personal and universal words of Teilhard de Chardin.*

'... I love you, Lord Jesus, because of the multitude who shelter within you and whom, if one clings closely to you, one can hear with all the other beings murmuring, praying, weeping ... I love you for the extensions of your body and soul to the farthest corners of creation through grace, through life, and through matter ... Lord Jesus, you who are as gentle as the human heart, as fiery as the forces of nature, as intimate as life itself, you in whom I can melt away and with whom I must have mastery and freedom: I love you as a world, as *this* world which has captivated my heart; and it is you, I now realize, that my brother men, even those who do not believe, sense and see through the magic immensities of the cosmos.

'... To live the cosmic life is to live dominated by the consciousness that one is an atom in the body of the mystical and cosmic Christ. The person who so lives dismisses as irrelevant a host of preoccupations that absorb the interest of other people. Such a person's life is open to larger horizons and such a person's heart is always more receptive. There you have my intellectual testament.'[126]

# 33

## BUT WHERE DO WE BEGIN? BEGIN WITH THE HEART – AND WITH THE SENSES

*Inner peace is closely related to care for ecology and for the common good because, lived out authentically, it is reflected in a balanced lifestyle together with a capacity for wonder which takes us to a deeper understanding of life ... it asks us to take time to recover a serene harmony with creation, reflecting on our lifestyle and our ideals, and contemplating the Creator who is within us and around us, whose presence 'must not be contrived but found, uncovered'.*
(EG 71) [LS 225]

We are focusing here on finding harmony within ourselves by falling in tune and timing with the pulse of nature, of the sky and of the sea. This, we feel sure, is where the regaining of a universal balance, healing and peace begins. And again, Pope Francis keeps reminding us that keeping these insights clear and fresh is the work of contemplation – of stilling the disturbing thoughts, of staying free of the anxious images, of becoming quiet enough to find a whole new perspective on what is going on in our lives. It is more like a dropping downwards, a sinking below the conscious waves of shallow mental effort. When we meditate, when we breathe into our restlessness and dis-ease, there is a perceptible shift in our self-awareness, and in the awareness of our isolation from our earthly home. This shift can happen quite quickly. It is an experience of tangible grace: it is the inner place to which Jesus went when it all became too much for him.

This way of seeing and of being is the way of Creation and Incarnation. It is the way of sacrament. It is the way of the mystics. It is the way of God. The basic rhythm and balance of our lives hold the key to our overall well-being, and to the well-being of the planet. Without the connected, contemplative heart our environmental efforts will be negligible. There will be no groundedness, rootedness or inner security, freedom or healing power within us. And therefore we will stay unaware of the ills of the Earth, disconnected from her pain, and unable to do anything to alleviate it. 'Inner peace is closely related to ecological concern' wrote the Pope. There are no shortcuts or cheap grace where saving the world is concerned.

Pope Francis tells us that an integral ecology includes 'taking time out to recover a serene harmony with creation'. To place oneself in the middle of creation, of what Rabindranath Tagore calls 'the stream of Life', what Krishnamurti calls 'the river of Life', is to feel a new power and perspective, a healthy confidence and balance in the current of one's destiny, even with all its alarming twists and turns, its many tiny trickles and mighty floods. The same flow of life that runs through my body night and day runs through the world, and dances in rhythmic measures. It is this same life that is rocked in the ocean-cradle of birth and of death, and in the ebb and flow in between. In this section of the encyclical the Pope is trying to achieve a far-reaching transformation in our consciousness – a profound deepening of our perception, an awareness of a Presence that pervades all things, not one we imagine or 'contrive', but one we actually 'find, uncover' at the core of everything.

To feel the power of the ocean during the day, to hear its muted murmur at night 'like a far wave' (Paul Murray), is to sense our intimacy with mystery. The sea, the senses, the soil, the seasons and the soul – all are related. They call to each other. They need each other because the soul needs a form, a shape and a context. The soul needs to be felt, named and experienced. This is why the spiritual is also physical – it spreads along the arteries of the embodied soul, through the timings and turnings of the universe itself. Moving to the tempo of the tides, and the pilgrimage of the clouds across the sky each morning, on a good day it is easy to visualise God's healing power touching our minds and caressing our troubled hearts and our troubled world.

The Pope knows our senses are sacred. When you listen carefully you can hear the silent music or the muted weeping of the Earth; when you look with attentiveness you notice the hidden loveliness of the most ordinary things; when you touch someone or something compassionately you bless and heal them – and yourself – with your graced presence. With his father St Francis and with his favourite poets, such as Gerard Manley Hopkins, the Pope asks us to let nature be our teacher. You get to realise more profoundly that you belong to something bigger than you; you remember that nature is the first Bible. In the turning of the seasons, in the waxing and waning of each day, nature's allure catches for you, reveals to you, and stirs within you the strains, traces and aches of an Astonishing Love.

## A FURTHER WORD

*In his encyclical Pope Francis is weaving together, as this book attempts to do, Creation, Incarnation, evolution – the inner dynamism and hidden work of the Risen One in each of us and in everything. A readiness to learn will draw and drive us to a deeper engagement with our suffering world, to an 'ecological conversion'.*

'Karl Rahner's theology makes it clear,' writes Judy Cannato, 'that we live in a world of grace, that we are created and constituted in love, and that love is the energy of evolution. This perspective gives a firm foundation from which to pose the questions that continue to arise. Grounded in human experience, Rahner's work reflects thoughtful dialogue between what we believe and the discoveries of science from which the Universe Story has emerged. With a profound grasp of the process of evolution, he begins weaving the two stories together for us. The whole of creation can be seen as a single movement, the one grace-filled self-communicating act of the God who can only be described as incomprehensible holy mystery. From the beginning God's intention has been to work through the evolution of the cosmos in such a way that creation itself comes to consciousness. Rooted in matter, creation has always evolved toward spirit, and in and through the human being – the universe coming to consciousness – spirit recognises itself ... Thus the Incarnation is not primarily about redemption from sin, but about coming to recognise our true nature.'[127]

# 34

## THE UNIVERSE AND ITS FAMILIES ARE GOD'S LOVE MADE VISIBLE

*The universe unfolds in God who fills it completely. Hence, there is a mystical meaning to be found in a leaf, in a mountain trail, in a dewdrop, in a poor person's face. The ideal is not only to pass from the exterior to the interior to discover the action of God in the soul, but also to discover God in all things. [LS 233]*

Pope Francis is clearly doing all he can in these reflections to convince us, without doubt, of the presence of divine love in everything that exists. He knows that we must keep falling in love with all aspects of Creation if we are ever to carry a devotion and reverence for its well-being. The encyclical inspires adults to recapture the wonderment of our inner child at the intricate mysteries of God's beautiful countenance to be found in a leaf, a trail, a face. This will lead to a renewed spirituality that will have its roots in a very ancient Celtic one.

Richard Rohr reminds us of the Buddhist understanding that God is the dynamic energy field of inter-being within which 'we live and move and have our being' (Acts 17: 28). There is one God 'above all things, through all things and in all things' (Ep 4: 6). And *as* all things. This ever-green presence can be fittingly imaged as a loving force field that influences and pervades everything, calling us to relationships of reconciliation and love, energising us to persevere in difficult times, reassuring us with hope when we are emptying ourselves in persevering service. For many of us, this vision and active commitment require a conversion of the soul so as to truly discover God in all things. This is a profound and necessary shift. It is called 'a transformed consciousness'.

From our innermost centre where the Blessed Trinity lives, and from the mysterious love pressing on us from all around, all we have to do is surrender to the truth of reality, to the embrace of the present moment, to the way things are. 'When you trust the river of life,' wrote Krishnamurti, 'the river of life has an astonishing way of taking care of you'. With practice this trusting becomes easier, this vibrant sensing of the healing heartbeat of God in the silent pulse of our attentive presence – the rhythm of our breathing, the rhythm of our being, the rhythm of God. Pope Francis wants us to discover another place of tranquillity inside us. Open to this God-Being, this overwhelming but shy and subtle presence, an extraordinary sense of peace and confidence may fill the soul. It is as though nature itself wants to empower us, reveal to us our inner, divine potential.

In 'Variation on a Theme by Rilke' Denise Levertov wrote:

> A certain day became a presence to me;
> There it was, confronting me – a sky, air, light;
> A being. And before it started to descend
> From the height of noon, it leaned over
> And struck my shoulder as if with
> The flat of a sword, granting me
> Honour and a task. The day's blow
> Rang out, or it was I, a bell awakened,
> And what I heard was my whole self
> Saying and singing what it knew: I CAN.[128]

In a footnote to the this extract (233) Pope Francis continues to persuade us of the divine beauty of every moment, of every experience of each of our senses. He draws on the beautiful words of Ali al-Khawas, a 9th-century Sufi mystic and poet. The Pope reaches for these perceptive expressions of incarnate holiness to capture his own vision of the fleshing of God's love, but also to win over our hearts to the true wonder of Christian teaching. 'There is a subtle mystery in each of the movements and sounds of this world. The beginner will capture what is being said when the wind blows, the trees sway, water flows, flies buzz, doors creak, or in the sound of strings or flutes, the sighs of the sick, the groans of the afflicted.'

Notice again the Pope's respect for the mysticism at the core of all the great religions. Out of his own experience the poet al-Khawas finds an intimacy with God in his closeness to the creatures of the world. St Bonaventure teaches that 'contemplation deepens the more we feel the working of God's grace within our hearts and the more we learn to encounter God in creatures outside ourselves'. There is but the one source of Being for all Creation, one life-giving Spirit that pervades everything that exists, whether it be the wings of a starling, the fall of a leaf, the flow of a stream, the beating of a heart. One of the names we give that mystery is God – the everyday God, that tender 24/7 Mother-Creator, whose love waves in every branch swaying in the autumn winds, and flows in every silent river winding its way to the sea.

## A FURTHER WORD

*This time of an unprecedented emergence of scientific discovery, of the renewal of a lost mysticism in our daily spirituality, together with the arrival on the scene of a Pope with huge spiritual incarnational vision and a 'magnanimous' heart, is both marking and offering a universal awakening and growth of the Spirit in each person and in the world itself. The best we can hope for in this life is to get the occasional glimpse. And a glimpse will do.*

'For Teilhard, God's creative action takes place through the immense evolutionary process in the universe. Human beings are an integral part of this process, shaped and moulded by universal energies, but in turn they themselves also contribute and help to shape the direction of this process. Human efforts assist in building up the body of God, the divine kingdom. The struggles of the universe reach into the most hidden parts of our being so that, given the power to see, we can recognize God's action through all events and things in our lives. Thus life becomes, for the believer, one long act of living communion with the incarnate Word and with God's creative action ... More than most, Teilhard was early aware that we are standing at the threshold of a new era, living in a new kind of society, globally interlinked, with our former geocentric, anthropocentric, and Eurocentric illusions being replaced by a new vision of the world. Few perceived this radical shift in human consciousness so acutely and so early in the twentieth century ...

‘ ... Teilhard also believed that the fundamentally psychic and spiritual nature of evolution is linked to a rise in inwardness and the growth of the spirit. He realized that inner energies were needed for human evolution to move forward and upward, toward a higher plane. He was always concerned with feeding the zest for living, for building the earth, for developing a planetary society with more equality, peace, and justice for all. To maintain the taste for life and feed the zest for living can never simply be taken for granted, just as we cannot take our health as a simple given but have to examine, cultivate, and take care of it. Zest for life is especially needed at the current stage when evolution has become conscious of itself in the self-reflective experience of human beings.’[129]

# 35

## OUR LIVED LIVES ON OUR EVOLVING PLANET ARE OUR DAILY INTIMACIES WITH GOD

*St John of the Cross taught that all the goodness present in the realities and experiences of this world 'is present in God eminently and infinitely, or more properly, in each of these sublime realities is God'. 'The mystic experiences the intimate connection between God and all beings,' he said, 'and thus feels that all things are God'. Standing awestruck before a mountain, they cannot separate this experience from God.*
[LS 234]

A heart-understanding of any one of these lyrical passages would radically change and deepen the meaning of our faith. It would lead us into a whole other delighted way of living our lives. These passages are richly incarnational and moving. We are here in the land of the mystic, a countryside too long denied to Christian believers, hidden behind edifices of correct doctrines and liturgical rubrics. These have their place, of course, but they are utterly secondary. Here in the Pope's words there is the food for which the heart aches, healthy nourishment for the emotions. The mystical core of Christianity (and of all the world's main religions) fires up a free and holistic energy in the human spirit.

This incarnate spirit of God is experienced not only in the most artistic, creative, beautiful and sublime moments and allurements, but in all that our senses drink in on our daily rounds. Notice the intensity of St John of the Cross's language and poetic imagery (see also his *Dark Night of the Soul*). As with the saint, our humanity will forever be reaching outwards and inwards for its completion in the heart of something much greater and fulfilling. It is a definition of our identity – that restless, daily yearning for some kind of belonging to a greater love.

There is a place within you called your 'mystical heart'. It is always searching for hidden beauty. It is that part of you that loves to wonder, to reflect deeply about the meaning of everything – the way things grow, how healing happens, how our bodies work, how our planet turns around the sun, how space seems infinite, how the divine fingerprints are on every particle of matter; it is that part of you that reflects deeply on how evolution has shaped you, how every cell in your body is a hymn to heaven and a declaration of love. Your amazing heart is capable of captivating insights into this Great Mystery. Here are two. Brian Swimme wrote that 'the earth was once molten rock – and now sings operas!' Hindu swami Prabhavananda wrote that 'the little space within the heart is as great as the vast universe. The Creator of heaven and earth is there, and the sun and the moon and the stars. Fire and lightning and winds are there, all that makes a human being is there ...'.

St John of the Cross is a grounded ascetic. No flights of fancy for him! Yet the Pope quotes him to bring home to us something of the warm vehemence of a soul in love with God, of a heart on fire with the desire for divine intimacy, and of the power of our senses and of nature to fuel that fire. 'Mountains have heights and they are plentiful, vast, beautiful, graceful, bright and fragrant. These mountains are what my Beloved is to me. Lonely valleys are quiet pleasant cool, shady and flowing with fresh water ... a delight to the senses ... These valleys are what my Beloved is to me.' (LS 234)

In this part of the encyclical Pope Francis seems really keen that we should understand the total accessibility of God's presence in our everyday, 'ordinary' lives. Even if we wanted to we would be hard put to avoid the experience of 'the Beloved'. It is practically inescapable. We cannot help coming into the embrace of divine compassion whenever we experience *anything*. 'We do not sometimes have experiences of love, fear, beauty or anything else, and then *also* have experiences of God,' writes Karl Rahner. 'No, the basic, original experience of God, on the contrary, is the ultimate depth and radical essence of *every personal* experience ...'. He goes on to say that if we cannot see and experience God in the ordinary events of life, we cannot expect to see and experience God when we gather for sacramental worship. For example, before the Sunday Eucharist can be a celebration of spiritual and joyful healing and empowerment, every human encounter with nature, with others, must be *felt* as a loving encounter with God.[130]

The extracts above from St John's writings are breathtakingly beautiful love poems. How wonderful to find them in an encyclical! From their ineffable abundance, in 'spousal symbols' and metaphors, they pour out their secrets and mysteries in lyrical language. After all, God did become human flesh with human senses. Rational dogma alone cannot handle the holistic impact of this revelation. We need a language of the heart – one that is expressed in elegant poetry, in words of a living, intimate flame burning in the purifying dark night of the soul. Remember the Pope's own mystical moment of light and darkness on the very day of his election to the papacy.

That strange experience of both peace and foreboding left its mark on him. He knows that an experience of God is at the heart of our faith, and that we all have such moments of 'being-in-love', of being passionately caught up in some dream or passion, without, perhaps, necessarily linking them with God's incarnate presence at all. In this encyclical the Pope relies on the mystics and artists to provide the connection between all our loves and God's love, to tell us about a God who fell in love with us, who created us so as to love us – and we can do nothing about it except gratefully accept it. All of this belongs to the kind of enchanted stories that capture the hearts of children – and our own! 'Once upon a time there was a lonely God ... '

## A FURTHER WORD

*The word 'grace' is mentioned a lot throughout these pages. It is a beautiful word that is often misused. Grace is not something we need more of. It is not a static entity that we can have a little or a lot of. Nor can we merit, earn or acquire it in any way. Grace is the dynamic, transformative*

*power in a vibrant Christian and evolutionary faith. It is*
*the purest of gifts. All we can do is accept the gift gratefully*
*with full hearts – or miss it completely. Grace is the way*
*we live out our lives with a sacramental understanding of*
*everything, with a rich imagination, and a wholehearted*
*surrender, deeply in love with God and with God's world.*

'Faith, as we understand it, is not, of course, simply the intellectual adherence to Christian dogma. It is taken in a much richer sense to mean belief in God charged with all the trust in his beneficent strength that the knowledge of the divine Being arouses in us. It means the practical conviction that the universe, between the hands of the Creator, still continues to be the clay in which he shapes innumerable possibilities according to his will ... Because we have believed intensely and with a pure heart in the world, the world will open the arms of God to us. It is for us to throw ourselves into these arms so that the divine milieu should close around our lives like a circle. That gesture of ours will be one of an active response to our daily task. *Faith consecrates the world.*'[131] Believing and becoming that consecration, that divine milieu, is the gift and work of grace.

# 36

## SACRAMENTS REVEAL AND CELEBRATE THE HIDDEN BEAUTY ALREADY IN THE WORLD

*The sacraments are a privileged way in which nature is taken up by God to become a means of mediating supernatural life. Water, fire, oil and colours are taken up in all their symbolic power and incorporated in our act of praise. The hand that blesses is an instrument of God's and a reflection of the closeness of Jesus Christ ... Encountering God does not mean fleeing from this world or turning our back on nature. [LS 235]*

The Word became flesh; it became nature; it became the universe. Creation and evolution are called a holy scripture, a central element in our knowing, loving and experiencing God. That is the whole point, for the Christian, of Incarnation. Nature is a sacrament of divine presence. The whole world is 'a sacrament of communion'. The human body is a sacrament of invisible beauty. Pope Francis wants us to understand this consequence of Incarnation – that everything is a sacrament, beginning with Creation itself. The sacraments are not only seven signs of God's special presence at significant times of our lives – they are the profound guarantee that God's grace is hidden in every moment, event, experience of our lives, indeed of all that is created. Everything in fact is sacrament. Or potentially so.

The first step towards a deeper understanding of sacraments – the three, or seven in particular, or sacramentality in general – is to see them in the context of a world already permeated and filled with God's presence. Grace is oriented to our humanity in its fullness. The 'holy' life can be lived only in the context of everyone's everyday existence. The seven sacraments in a specially focused way keep reminding us of this revelation. In time and space, in ordinary signs and symbols – 'water, fire, oil, colours' – the scattered fragments of our lives are gathered up to remind us of their their sublime meaning in the light of Christ. Professor John Macquarrie writes, 'In word and sacrament, the divine presence is focussed so as to communicate itself to us with a directness and intensity like that of the Incarnation itself ...'.[132]

Gregory Baum, a *peritus* at Vatican II, writes, 'The radical distinction between the sacred and the secular has been overcome in the person of Christ. In Christ it is revealed that the locus of the divine is the human. The Christian way of worship, then, can no longer consist in sacred rites by which people are distanced from the ordinary circumstances of their lives. Christian liturgy is, rather, the celebration of the deepest dimensions of human life, which is God's way of communicating the divine self to people. Liturgy unites people more closely with their daily lives. Sacramental worship remembers and celebrates the marvellous things God works in the lives of people, purifies and intensifies these gifts, making people more sensitive to the Word and Spirit present in their secular context.'[133]

In light of the fact of evolution and a developing theology, our understanding of the seven sacraments needs new exploring – and imagination. Seen against the expanding horizons of Creation and Incarnation, of nature and grace, of science and theology, we might understand baptism, for instance, as the celebration of the miracle of all birth, the blessing of Creation and life itself, the entering into a world community, all of whom are God's people. It is not about initiation into the Roman Catholic Institution by exorcising the devil out of the innocent child. It has a richer, deeper, more beautiful meaning. 'We belong to God's family from the first moment of our existence. Christian faith and baptism are a response to a call to belong *in this particular way* to the family of God by belonging to the community of Jesus. To be baptised is not to enter the world of grace, because the grace and love of God is already there; it is freely given, it surrounds our existence, and we are all imbued with it from the first moment of our conception. But to be initiated into the family of Jesus is a matter of entering into a conscious process in which the experience of dying and rising becomes the pattern for one's life-style'.[134]

Baptism is a sacrament of evolution. It is the threshold to participation in the New Universe story and the possibility of a new future for the cosmos. It is the sacrament of utter wonder at the baby's beauty, and at the sublime creativity of the Mother-God whose artistry and imagination it was that this tiny mite would be created. It is the sacrament also of the very beginning of life itself, of that first 'Flaring Forth', of that Big Bang nearly 14 billion years ago, and of that long infancy called evolution that has brought another wee human being onto this planet. And the baby Jesus before that. All are children of the cosmos, the living gold dust of the stars, small bodies of God. 'Yes,' exclaims Thomas Berry (to the new baby), 'You *are* that star, brought into a form of life that enables life to reflect on itself. The star *does* know of its great work, of its surrender to allurement, of its stupendous contribution to life, but only through its further articulation – you!' Small wonder the universe shivers with delight when we gather around the baptismal font to honour the divinity of the baby from its first breath, and before.

## A FURTHER WORD

*This reflection is a reminder that before looking at the 'seven sacraments' in this richer way, we need to confidently understand the very notion of sacrament in general, of sacramentality, as when the Pope writes of 'the whole world as sacrament'. This extremely important. Without this broader vision, this wider window, we will struggle to understand Incarnation, or the personal and cosmic reality of an evolving universe. Catholic Christians celebrate the very love, meaning and mystery of Creation and Incarnation every time they sit and sing around the table of bread and truth. Do you feel the tingle of a deeper understanding when you read (below) about the part we play in the consecration of the whole evolving universe of joys and suffering of all life each sacramental Sunday morning?*

'... And then there appears to the dazzled eyes of the believer the Eucharistic mystery itself, extended infinitely into a veritable universal transubstantiation in which the words of the consecration are applied not only to the sacrificial bread and wine but, mark you, to the whole mass of joys and sufferings produced by the convergence of the world as it progresses. And it is then, too, that there follow in consequence the possibilities of a universal communion ... God can in the future be experienced and apprehended (and can even, in a true sense, be completed) by the whole ambient totality of what we call evolution – *in Christo Jesu* ...'.[135]

'How strange, my God, are the processes your spirit initiates! What I discern in your breast is simply a furnace of fire; and the more I fix my gaze on its ardency the more it seems to me that all around it the contours of your body melt away and become enlarged beyond all measure, till the only features I can distinguish in you are those of the face of a world which has burst into flame ... For me, my God, all joy and all achievements, the very purpose of my being and all my love of life, all depend on this one basic vision of the union between yourself and the universe. Let others, fulfilling a function more august than mine, proclaim your splendours as pure spirit; as for me, dominated as I am by a vocation which springs from the inmost fibers of my being, I have no desire, I have no ability to proclaim anything except the innumerable prolongations of your incarnate being in the world of matter; I can preach only the mystery of your flesh, you the soul shining forth through all that surrounds us.'[136]

# 37

## YOUR TRUE HUMAN PRESENCE IS WHERE GOD'S INCARNATE PRESENCE IS DISCLOSED

*'Beauty, which in the East is one of the best loved names expressing divine harmony and transfigured humanity, appears everywhere – in lights and sounds and colours and scents'. For Christians all the creatures of the material universe find their true meaning in the incarnate Word, planting in them a seed of definitive transformation ... bodiliness is considered in all its value in the liturgical act whereby the human body is disclosed in its inner nature as a temple of the Holy Spirit ...'*
(Pope St John Paul II) [LS 235]

Again, notice the rich rapture and sublime depth of the words here. Images and evocative phrases pile up. So many profound dimensions of spirituality are packed into one paragraph – the notion of beauty, of God's seed in everything, of the divinity of the human body, of the wonder of the Word made Flesh. For a start, the Pope, by quoting Pope St John Paul II, is suggesting that we need to recover the notion of beauty. Why? Because few things have the compelling power of beauty in all its million shapes and forms. It beckons to us, and points beyond itself. We know it is a sacrament of God because that is what the beautiful humanity of Jesus is.

Beauty awakens us to our own mystery, made as we are in God's image, and transforms us more deeply into it. For beauty we are born. By beauty we are nourished. From beauty we came. In an article entitled 'The Transforming Power of Beauty' Ronald Rolheiser reminds us that, being fashioned from the 'Imago Dei', we already know beauty and carry it within us. He refers to 'that deep virginal spot within us, that place where hands infinitely more gentle that our own once caressed us before we were born, where our souls were kissed before birth, where all that is most precious in us still dwells, where the fire of love still burns – in that place we feel a *vibration sympathetique* in the face of true beauty. It stirs the soul where it is most tender' (25 June 1999).

In our essential experience of beauty we are touching the heart of God. This is a moment of a sense of heaven. The soul of the whole world, from its very beginning, is kept vibrantly alive by the pulse of beauty. In that sense, whether we know it or not, whether we are religious or not, we are, the Christian would say, living in the heart of God, 'taken up into it' (*EG* 178). In the appreciation, wonder, sharing and experience of what is truly beautiful, no one is excluded. All become one in the community of beauty. No one has the special pass, or code for club membership. This is probably what Pope Francis is saying about beauty. In believers' terms, against the backdrop of the Incarnation, does it ever make sense to talk about 'secular' beauty, about the 'secular world of the arts', about a 'godless world', about 'merely human' beauty? Where true beauty is, God is. Since the Incarnation there are not two levels of beauty. So, for instance, a community may be churchless, religion-less too, but not 'Godless' or 'beauty-less'.

In *Waiting on God* Simone Weil wrote the wonderfully succinct sentence, 'Like a sacrament, the beauty of the world is Christ's tender smile for us coming through matter.' Always drawn towards God, we carry an unconscious attraction towards becoming a 'small reflection', as St Paul put it, of that beautiful smile. 'We do not only want to see beauty,' wrote C. S. Lewis in *The Weight of Glory*, 'we want something else that can hardly be put into words – to unite with the beauty we see, to pass into it, to receive it into ourselves, to bathe in it, to become part of it'. In a previous letter Pope Francis wrote about 'teaching something beautiful, capable of filling life with new splendour and profound joy in the midst of difficulties. *Every* expression of true beauty can thus be acknowledged as a path leading to an encounter with God ... [therefore] we must be bold enough to discover new signs and new symbols, new flesh to embody and communicate the

Word, and different forms of beauty which are valued in different cultural settings ...' (*EG* 167)

The human body is a mirror where the secret world of the soul comes to expression. It is a sacred threshold, 'the temple of the Holy Spirit' referred to in baptism. The sensuous is sacred, the body is truthful. The mind may deceive you; the body cannot. It is your safest home all your life – and God's home too. There is a false dualism between body and mind. They are as one. The soul is not hidden within the body; your body is in your soul and both will live on in heaven. In spite of the tragically flawed and radically destructive teaching about our bodies as the punishment of God for our non-existent first parents' 'original sin', and our eviction from a non-existent garden, Pope St John Paul II offers a most beautiful comment on what is really our Divine Mother-Artist's most beautiful works of art.

'The body, in fact,' he writes, 'and only the body, is capable of making visible what is invisible, the spiritual and the divine. It was created to transfer into the visible reality of the world the mystery hidden from eternity in God, and thus be a sign of it ... In man, created in the image of God, the very sacramentality of creation, the sacramentality of the world, was, in some way, revealed. In fact, through his bodiliness, his masculinity and femininity, man becomes a visible sign of the economy of Truth and Love, which has its source in God himself and was revealed already in the mystery of creation.'[137] The light in our bodies is the same light that shone at the transfiguration of Jesus, the same light that flared forth from the fire of the Big Bang. Our history is one long, unbroken and beautiful story of an astonishing, suffering love.

## A FURTHER WORD

*'Our human nature, its being and its presence, is the greatest of all the sacraments in revealing God's mystery and incarnate reality.' Not even the angels could say that! Only humans. Our very 'bodiliness', Pope Francis insists*

> (LS 235), is the clearest window into the divine beauty.
> He affirms this with confidence because God chose to be
> revealed in the first Creation, and then in a human being.
> Jesus told St Teresa that without our bodies and senses God
> could achieve nothing. St Augustine used almost the very
> same words. Music and dance, for instance, play a huge
> part in making the invisible visible, the intangible tangible.
> The Incarnation was, and is, the feast of the body; it cel-
> ebrates the flesh; it honours the senses as the thresholds of
> the divine. It is in the body that we experience heaven; and
> it is in the body that God experiences the earth.

'A flamenco dancer, lurking under the shadow, prepared for the terror of her dance. Somebody had wounded her in words, alluding to the fact that she had no fire, or *duende*. She knows she has to dance her way past her limitations, and that this may destroy her forever ... When the music starts she begins to dance, with ritual slowness. Then she stamps out the dampness from her soul. Then she stamps fire into her loins. She takes on a strange enchanted glow. With dark tragic rage, shouting, she hurls her hungers, her doubts, her terrors and her secular prayers for more light into the spaces around her. Soon she becomes a wild unknown force, glowing in her death, dancing from her wound, dying in her dance.'[138] Ben Okri wrote this story about what happens when the sensual human being is fired by the inner power of the spirit of life.

The Christian will call this the work of the Holy Spirit, a power described by the Church Fathers as the *perichoresis* of the Blessed Trinity deep in our souls. Richard Rohr translates that Greek word as 'God's circle-dance of communion' in our hearts. I wonder if Pope Francis had anything like Okri's image in mind when he wrote of the Spirit's inner temple in each human body, of the flesh as 'the hinge of salvation', as Church Father Tertullian and Pope St John Paul II put it, and the sacred dance of the liturgical celebration (235).

# 38

## THE FIERCE UNIVERSE OF BLAZING LOVE IN A FRAGILE WAFER ON OUR TONGUE

*It is in the Eucharist that all that has been created finds its greatest exaltation ... The Lord, in the culmination of the mystery of the incarnation, chose to reach our intimate depths through a fragment of matter. He comes, not from above, but from within; he comes to be found by us in this world of ours ... Joined to the incarnate Son, present in the Eucharist, the whole cosmos gives thanks to God. Indeed the Eucharist is itself an act of cosmic love. [LS 236]*

Please try to understand the beautiful theology here. You already sense it in your hearts. Reflect on the meaning of 'sacramentality' – the notion that everything is a potential revelation of God. Everything! And each creature finds its fulfilment in God. The Eucharist, 'in a fragment of matter' penetrates, gathers up and embraces all Creation. Human, non-human and all created entities form a single spiritual community, each worshipping God in its own way. It should not be revolutionary or radical to say that every creature is destined for salvation in Christ. And that all will sit around the same table. At one shining moment, 'in that new world where the fullness of your peace will be revealed, gather people of every race, religion, language and way of life to share in the one eternal banquet ...' (Eucharistic Prayer for Children II). May that 'new world' be this world transformed, and may that dream of the future start happening soon!

Good theology reminds us that everything that is true of the Incarnation is true of the Eucharist. This is a grace-filled insight that enriches, deepens and en-graces our celebration of the sacrament. In the form of bread and wine, humanity offers back to God what is God's own, and time and space are sanctified. Beyond a very individualistic explanation of 'going to Mass' and mostly irrelevant arguments about the rubrics of it, Pope Francis and his two predecessors ask us to open our minds to a magnificently richer understanding of what our Sunday celebration means. It is a holy communion of heaven and earth, a moment of true vision of the divinity of our human lives, a time for the whole universe to sing a song of thanks to its Creator, an experience of the abundant and eternal horizon – all somehow focused on a piece of bread. The Kingdom that is to come, the Omega we strive for, is already around us. This Earth, the whole universe, in the light of Incarnation, is a kind of theophany of God's Real Presence. We are living now in that astonishing milieu where we perceive every sensation of every sense as the touch and whisper of God!

Every Eucharist is a confirmation, a guarantee, a divine assurance, a celebration of the intrinsic meaning of the Incarnation – that matter and spirit are now one – and always have been; all nature is forever graced; to be truly human is to be divine. This is the good news that your heart is longing for, that your spirit thirsts for before beginning another week of your life with its passions, pains and paradoxes. This utter humanising of God in flesh, bread and wine sounds shocking to many. No other religion teaches anything like it. We are not saved by doctrines, scriptures, religions, pilgrimages and rituals alone. God comes to feed us – people of the flesh – primarily in the earthy and unique intimacy of food. And we do not just look at it. We touch, taste, eat and drink it. This is because the Mass is Incarnation in miniature. Divine love takes the intimate shape of our essential, sensual, raw selves. When we sit at the table of truth, love and beauty, immediately after receiving Holy Communion, we hear the vital whisper of assurance: 'I am now the living food of your flesh. I am the vibrant wine of your energy, the power within you. In me you are made complete, and you are invincible even in your darkest winter. And when your heart is full, it will overflow into other hungry hearts.'

Among Pope Francis's most memorable 'asides' is his comment about the generous hospitality of the Eucharist. It is to be eaten as a healing medicine for all those of us who are sick in some way, rather than as the banquet reward for those who have achieved perfection. It is free. It is welcoming. Only the hypocrites are critiqued. Nothing and nobody has the power to stop us from receiving Holy Communion once we hunger for it. Countless Catholics, for one reason or another, consider themselves unworthy to receive at Mass. Or they are told that they are. But the gospels tell them a different story – that God is the freely offered food 'for all' *without exception*. All we have to provide is the hunger. 'Christ is the bread,' wrote St Augustine, 'awaiting hunger'. When we make the Eucharistic meal into anything else – something, for example, to define membership – we are on the verge of sinning against the Incarnation. 'Too often,' writes Richard Rohr, 'we use the Eucharist to separate who's in from who's out, who's worthy from who's unworthy, instead of to declare that all of us are radically unworthy, and that worthiness is not even the issue. The issue is about surrender and hunger. And, more often, sinners are hungrier than "saints".'

God's extraordinary desire for us has never ever dimmed or faded in the intensity of its burning. It is in the ordinariness, accessibility and saving blessing of bread that this ravishing love incarnate is experienced and celebrated. And it is in the sacramentality of the celebration that a most comforting truth is revealed; in all our daily efforts to be human and loving, Eucharistic grace is always surrounding us, enfolding us, empowering and consecrating us. R. S. Thomas ended his poem 'The Moor' with these sublime words:

> ... I walked on,
> Simple and poor, while the air crumbled
> And broke on me generously as bread [139]

## A FURTHER WORD

*If we do not recognise the face of the risen Christ in every face, if we do not identify every event, every experience as God's home, if we are not interested in our world as God's incarnate and evolving body, then, as theologian Karl Rahner says, there is little point in going to Mass on Sunday. He even calls it 'worthless'! How can we be convinced that this revolutionary teaching is true? To be sure, we all go to Mass for our own reasons. And they are all valid. But Rahner is trying to connect the Mass deeply to our daily lives, to see it as the place we listen to the Spirit of Love within us, that song of our most authentic heart; and to believe in the utterly extravagant, unconditional nature of God's immense love for us and for the multiverse miracles he/she made. Again, ponder on these words from the heart of de Chardin:*

'Since first, Lord, you said, *"Hoc est corpus meum"* (This is my Body), not only the bread of the altar but (to some degree) everything in the universe that nourishes the soul of the life of spirit and grace has become *yours* and has become *divine* – it is divinized, divinizing, and divinizable. Every presence makes me feel that you are near me; every touch is that touch of your hand; every necessity transmits to me a pulsation of your will. And so true is this, that everything around me that is essential and enduring has become for me the dominance and, in some way, the substance of your heart ...

'That is why it is impossible for me, Lord – impossible for any person who has acquired even the smallest understanding of you – to look on your face without seeing in it the *radiance* of every reality and every goodness. In the mystery of your mystical body – your cosmic body – you sought to feel the echo of every joy and every fear that moves each single one of all the countless cells that make up humankind. And correspondingly, we cannot contemplate you and adhere to you without your Being, for all its supreme simplicity, transmuting itself as we grasp it into the restructured multitude of all that you love upon earth ...

'When I think of you, Lord, I cannot say whether it is in this place that I find you more or in that place, whether you are to me a friend or strength or matter, whether I am contemplating you or whether I am suffering, whether I rue my faults or find union, whether it is you I love or the whole sum of others. Every affection, every desire, every possession, every light, every depth, every harmony, and every ardour glitters with equal brilliance, at one and the same time in the inexpressible *relationship* that is being set up between me and you ...'.[140]

# 39

## 'THIS IS MY BODY' – IT ECHOES ACROSS THE COSMOS OF OUR HEARTS AND THE HEART OF OUR COSMOS

*'Yes, cosmic! Because even when it is celebrated on the humble altar of a country church, the Eucharist is always, in some way, celebrated on the altar of the world.' The Eucharist joins heaven and earth; it embraces and penetrates all creation ... in the bread of the Eucharist 'creation is projected towards divinisation ... toward unification with the Creator himself'. (Ecclesia de Eucharistia, Pope St John Paul II; Corpus Christi homily – Pope Benedict XVI). [LS 236]*

As well as for our traditional reasons and personal needs, we are here invited to understand the Mass as also the sacramental moment of an astonishing revelation – the revelation of the love and meaning hidden in the first moment, in the first nano-second of Creation, the revelation of the burning 14 billion years of the presence of God warming and preparing the Earth as a cradle of welcome for humanity and for the Bethlehem infant; the revelation that the history of evolution is the genealogy and long cosmic gestation of that baby. In celebrating Eucharist, in receiving Holy Communion, we experience the soul of the Earth. The Eucharist encapsulates for ever this astonishing hymn of love at the core of the cosmos. In sacramental form, Thomas Berry holds, with bread and wine, the whole world is acknowledging and celebrating its very being as flowing from the womb of God at the beginning of time, and in each passing moment moving inevitably towards its divine fulfilment in Christ.

We can safely identify the Christ-story with the 'New Story of the Universe'. When we gather, pray and sing around the table of truth, we are contemplating the Eucharist as the deepest symbol of the hidden secrets already buried and burning in the core of Creation. We are liturgically expressing and celebrating the river of love that streamed out at the beginning of time, and now, and for ever, flows everywhere. That love sustains the cosmos of our hearts and the heart of our cosmos, 'groaning in one great act of giving birth', on their long journey home. That is why the physical world itself is the incarnate body of God and will enjoy the same future as we will. Theologian John Macquarrie explains that this profound understanding of salvation is repeated, clarified, purified and celebrated at every true Eucharistic gathering 'with a directness and an intensity like that of Incarnation itself'. The mighty mystery of universal existence is encapsulated in one ordinary daily sacramental moment. Every Mass is a cosmic event.

'Yes, cosmic!' Our Pope, as we saw (above), quotes from Pope St John Paul II's *Ecclesia de Eucharistia*: 'Because even when the Eucharist is celebrated on the humble altar of a country church, it is always, in some way, celebrated on the altar of the world. It embraces, permeates and celebrates all Creation' (8). In his 'Feast of Faith' he explains why 'Christian liturgy must be cosmic liturgy, why it must, as it were, orchestrate the mystery of Christ with all the voices of Creation'. These are such beautiful words from the saint when he writes from within his poetic soul. They liberate our own poetic souls to fly free into the truth of our imagination, that incarnate gift of God's own creativity. With it we explore the infinite depths of wisdom and beauty in that repeated gathering each Sunday, to celebrate 'out of our intimate depths' as Pope Francis puts it, glimpses of the utterly and eternally sublime vision that God has for each one of us, and for our Mother, the beautiful Earth from which we come.

At every moment, somewhere across our planet, the eternal words of disclosure are spoken: 'This is my Body'. They sound around the Earth and they echo among the stars. They were whispered by our loving Mother-God when the terrible beauty of the first fiery atoms shattered the infinite darkness with unimaginable flame and light. 'This is my Body.' It is God-become atom, become-galaxy, become-star, become-earth, become-universe, become-cosmos, become-human flesh, speaking these words of wonder to the whole of Creation in its own voice of gift and gratitude. It is a fire in our souls that is fanned to a new flame each Sunday, a fire that warms the community around us, the world we live in, the whirling universe that embraces us all.

In his poetic Eucharistic reflections, especially in his sublime *Hymn of the Universe*,[141] Teilhard de Chardin sees the sacramental species as formed by the totality of the world. This is a most profound, transforming and beautiful meditation.De Chardin perceives the duration of Creation, 'the growth of the world borne ever onwards', as the time needed for its completed consecration. The unfolding of the secrets of the phenomenon called life, in all its personal, earthy, cosmic dimensions, with its fearful darkness and irresistible brightness, is the bread and wine of God's universal becoming. Without the Mass we would surely forget that our beautiful God is very incarnate indeed!

We receive Holy Communion to really become the bread and wine, allowing them to transform our very being into the presence of God. And then, fully reflecting our baptismal ordination as priestesses and prophetesses of God, to continue consecrating, through our senses and very existence, every moment, action, experience of each day and night: as the mother consecrates each family breakfast and daily encounter, as the artist consecrates life with the gifts of insight and creativity, as travellers consecrate every field and lake and town with their compassionate eyes, as the scientists and astronauts bless the immensity we can only guess at, by their curiosity and admiration. The Eucharist reminds us that we are the original 'blessers', the forgivers of sins, the co-saviours of the world with God.

## A FURTHER WORD

*The silent, sacramental moment after receiving Holy Communion is the precious, timeless space when we touch and feel the mystery of love, when we open ourselves completely to the personal and universal presence of grace, when,*

> *inextricably fused with our Tremendous Lover, we become*
> *intimately aware that we are already that blessed presence*
> *in our communities. May the Holy Spirit clarify our hearts*
> *and minds to really grasp these truths and live by them.*

'Eucharist is the sacrament of life. The sacrament of my life – of my life received, of my life lived, of my life surrendered ... Because you ascended into heaven after having descended into hell, you have so filled the universe in every direction, Jesus, that henceforth it is blessedly impossible for us to escape you ... Now I know that for certain. Neither life, whose advance increases your hold upon me, nor death, which throws me into your hands, nor the good or evil spiritual powers, which are your living instruments, nor the energies of matter into which you have plunged, nor the irreversible stream of duration whose rhythm and flow you control without appeal, nor the unfathomable abysses of space which are the measure of your greatness ... none of these things will be able to separate me from your substantial love, because they are all only the veil, the "species," under which you take hold of me in order that I may take hold of you ... and grasp you in every creature. And so, that we should triumph over the world with you, come to us clothed in the glory of the world.'[142]

# 40

## HE IS MY SON; HE TAKES AFTER ME

*The Son ... united himself to this earth when he was formed in the womb of Mary (238) She treasures the entire life of Jesus in her heart. 'Son of God, Jesus, you were formed in the womb of Mary our Mother, you became part of this earth ... Today you are alive in every creature in your risen glory ...'*
(LS 241, 246; End-Prayer 2)

A key foundational core of Christianity is the humanity of Jesus Christ. This is the (shocking) heart of the faith for the Catholic Christian – that Jesus was utterly and totally an 'ordinary' human being. Without this historical moment there would be no Christian faith or church or scriptures, nor could this encyclical have been written. 'Jesus,' mused Pope Francis, 'worked with his hands, in daily contact with the matter created by God, to which he gave form by his craftsmanship. It is striking that most of his life was dedicated to this task in a simple life which awakened no admiration at all: "Is not this the carpenter, the son of Mary?"' (*LS* 98; see also *Gaudium et Spes*, Vatican II, 22). The Pope understands this truth as the central source of Christian revelation, and endeavours to highlight it throughout the encyclical, pointing out the sublime role of Mary in ensuring the 100 per cent humanity of Jesus – and therefore of God.

Mothers and their babies. What a human/divine mystery! What a real moment of uniquely human experience. While the orthodox teaching of the virgin birth lies at the core of so many Christian doctrines, the actual reality of that birth, for the baby to be genuinely human, would have revealed a very anxious, messy scene, untidy and unrehearsed. Maybe we need more images of a bawling, bloody infant struggling to find its breath, squeezing its eyes against the new light. The challenge here is to keep the doctrinal meaning in balance with the visceral experience of heart and gut. After all, it is *Incarnation* – a painful fleshing. It does seem strange that this unique moment of 'being human', of that most intense, tender and poignant experience of a mother and baby in the mystery of raw birth, is not perennially recaptured and celebrated in our incarnational, liturgical worship. God becomes a baby in the way of all babies, when human blood, flesh and seed are consecrated as the raw material for the birth of God.

How much of our mothers' essential soul and spirit do we catch off them when we're very small, how much of their light and shadow? And how much are mothers aware of the unique and divine mystery they incarnate in their offspring? 'Once a woman has carried her baby inside her body for nine months and brought it forth through the pain of childbirth,' writes Richard Rohr, 'she knows something about mystery, about miracles, and about transformation that men will never know'. Hans Urs von Balthasar, theologian of beauty and favourite of Pope Benedict, tries to describe this human/divine dynamic: 'After a mother has smiled for a long time at her child, the child will begin to smile back. She has awakened love in its heart, and in this awakening love, she awakens also recognition.' This is how Jesus was made aware of joy and love – and thus of God. All utterly through his mother. The divine sonship of Jesus had very human beginnings. And the poet Rainer Maria Rilke believed that an infant's journey into human awareness depended on the beckoning, beguiling voice of the mother, 'easing the child into self-hood, lessening the shadows of the abyss that trap us in inarticulate darkness'.

As with all mothers Mary would have carried, formed and nourished Jesus for nine months in her womb. How much of her very being would have been visible in him? Working, eating, sleeping, Mary was forming Jesus' body from her own – his features, his limbs and his human/divine powers. Did he have her colouring, her eyes, her smile, her way of walking? Would the neighbours have said, 'For sure, that's Mary's boy – just look at the freckles on his nose.' Atheist Jean Paul Sartre imagines Mary looking at her newborn son and thinking, 'This God is my son. The divine flesh is my flesh. He is made from me. He has my eyes, and the shape of his mouth is the shape of mine. He takes after me. He is God, and he takes after me. No other woman has ever had her God fall to her lot in this way. A small God whom I can take in my arms and cover with kisses. A warm God who breathes and smiles. A God who lives and whom I can touch.' Holding him and gazing at him with tender power she sowed the seeds of an immense courage in his heart. Was it through his mother that he experienced the security, intimacy and tender feminine energy that empowered his divine ministry? And at that last moment on the cross, bereft and hopeless, did his desperate eyes catch the quiet intensity in his mother's uplifted face, and did those memories once again burn through his despair and bless his breaking heart?

The human love of Jesus was the divine love of God. So is ours. His forgiveness was the forgiveness of God. So is ours. How did Jesus know this? He knew it because of his mother. He drank in that wisdom with her milk. It was on her lap that his 'inner authority' was nurtured. His capacity for intimate relationships began with the gaze of delight between him and his mother as he guzzled greedily at her breast. Later, when his fear terrified him, it was his mother's eyes he remembered; when his doubts unbalanced him, it was her touch that restored his trust, and when the devil bedazzled him, it was her warm embrace that renewed his confidence. Let mothers tell us about Incarnation.

## A FURTHER WORD

*Amongst a million implications of Incarnation, the human-ity of God and the femininity of God are central. The Institutional Church is slow to embrace either of these rev-elations concerning the utter equality of divine love for all humanity. Again and again this attitude is emphasised in the stubborn exclusion of women from any of the major orders of ordination. One can only conclude, with a certain shock, that the radical meaning of true and deep Incarna-tion has been neglected by the Roman Catholic Institution throughout the history of its existence.*

All the way to Elizabeth
and in the months afterward,
she wove him, pondering,
'This is my body, my blood.'

Beneath the watching eyes
of donkey, ox and sheep
she rocked him, crooning,
'This is my body, my blood.'

In the moonless desert flight
and the Egypt-days of his growing
she nourished him, singing,
'This is my body, my blood.'

Under the blood-smeared cross
she rocked his mangled bones,
remembering him, moaning,
'This is my body, my blood.'

When darkness, stones and tomb
bloomed to Easter morning,
she ran to him, shouting,
'This is my body, my blood.'

And no one thought to tell her:
'Woman , it is not fitting
for you to say those words.
You don't resemble him.'[143]

# 41

## THE WORLD IS A WEB OF LOVE. WE CANNOT ESCAPE IT. WE ARE IT! OUR LIFE IS DIVINE

*... the world, created according to the divine model, is a web of relationships. Creatures tend towards God, and in turn it is proper to every living being to tend towards other things, so that throughout the universe we can find any number of constant and secretly interwoven relationships. This leads us not only to marvel at the many connections existing among creatures but also discovering a key to our own fulfilment ... Everything is interconnected and this invites us to develop a spirituality of that global solidarity which flows from the mystery of the Trinity. [LS 240]*

Creation is a web of relationships – a kind of mystical body. Everything in the universe is connected. We are all one, all part of the One Energy Field, the One Creative Source, the One Loving Creator. You, and the Earth you live in, are the Spirit's beauty in matter and flesh, conspiring to make the 'dream of the Earth' come true. Eternal Love is expressing itself through you, *as* you and as the world itself. With the Loving Mystery, in stone, star and soul, you are the co-creator of the future. You have the Creator's power to become who you are meant to be, to evolve towards the final Omega of life. Be ever-ready, expectant, open to the gracious call of the Final Intimacy. These empowering teachings and truths will sustain you on your journey. 'We all flow from one source,' wrote Judy Cannato. 'There is a single Creator who remains present to every person and every part of the cosmos, sustaining and empowering their on-going development. Some will call that process evolution; others the work of the Spirit.'[144]

The notion of the universe as a sacrament of intercommunion and interconnectedness is a constant, pressing and central teaching of

Pope Francis. It is emphasised many times throughout his encyclical: 'our conviction that, as part of the universe, called into being by one Father, all of us are linked by unseen bonds and together form a kind of universal family, a sublime communion which fills us with a sacred affectionate and humble respect'. When he refers to 'the divine model' he means the Trinitarian context of intimate expanding relationships: God, the Mother of Life (Parent, Source, Eternal Love), Son, the Human One (made flesh, incarnate Love), and the Holy Spirit (the Love-Energy, the free and flowing force in all evolving life). Notice the incarnational, evolutionary theme –'web of relations', 'throughout the universe we can find any number of constant and secretly woven relationships', 'everything is interconnected'. Even though we struggle to understand the mysterious workings of evolution, and to experience 'that Trinitarian dynamism which God imprinted' in all created and uncreated being, yet we are stirred by excitement and wonder when we ponder the nature of that primordial oneness imaged and described as a flowing, an awakening, a dancing, an allurement, a loving, a creating, a returning.

In the first ever papal TED talk ('The Future of You', April 2017) Pope Francis quoted John Donne's famous reflection, reminding us that 'no man is an island, entire of itself'. All our lives are inseparably involved with one another; through innumerable interactions they are forever linked together. No one lives alone. The lives of others continually spill over into mine – in what I think, do, say, achieve. And, conversely, my life spills over into that of others, for better and for worse. There is an Irish phrase that reflects the same truth – Ar scath a chéile a mhaireann na daoine (people live in each other's shadow). As Dostoevsky put it, 'We are all responsible to everyone for everything.'

In *The Unbearable Wholeness of Being: God, Evolution and the Power of Love* Ilia Delio writes that every human being desires to love and to be loved, to belong to another, because we come from another. We are born social and relational. We yearn to belong, to be part of a larger whole that includes not only friends and family but neighbours, community, trees, flowers, sun, earth, stars. 'We are born of nature and are part of nature; that is, we are born into a web of life and are part of a web of life.'[145]

Evolution is not some distant background to the human story; it is *your* story – the slow, painful love story of your conception in the heart of Love. Brian Swimme says, 'We awake to a universe permeated with love; we spend our time learning how to become this love.' And Richard Rohr believes that 'love is the energy of the entire universe, from orbiting protons and neutrons to the orbiting of planets and stars. This indwelling love is a wounded love, forever calling to us with urgent cries. And deep in our DNA we belong to the stars, the trees, the galaxies. We belong to one another because we have the same source of love; the love that flows through the trees is the same love that flows through my being ... We are deeply connected in this flow of love, beginning on the level of nature where we are the closest of kin because the earth is our mother.'[146] Whenever we glimpse that revelation, and try to live it in 'right relationship with all creation', in love with all creatures, then we are playing our necessary part in saving the world. Dylan Thomas expresses this interfusion of nature and grace as only the poet can. We repeat his comprehensive words:

> The force that through the green fuse drives the flower
> Dries my green age ...
> The force that drives the water through the rock
> Drives my red blood.[147]

## A FURTHER WORD

*'In a straight line, and alone, nobody goes very far' (Antoine de Sainte-Exupéry). Creation and Incarnation are continuous; yet our understanding of both mysteries has scarcely begun; and we are all playing a part in the development or diminishment of that unique story. Does it now seem as*

*though a radical change in our understanding of our faith is a real choice – where individual salvation and escape from this threatening world are no longer the point of our existence; only a bigger and infinitely more beautiful and compassionate love story that captures our hearts with an extraordinary happiness?*

'[It is so important to remember] that human nature is, and of itself, an incomplete, ever-evolving thing. We are still on the way toward becoming fully human, both as individual persons and collectively, as a species. Deep down inside us there is a hunger – a basic fundamental drive – toward something that is not yet. We see it around us – the urge for fulfilment, for completeness, for all-togetherness. We see it in sexuality. We see it in the arts and the search for lasting beauty. We see it in the search for complete knowledge and with the quest for "a theory of everything" ... The same impulse, the same quest for unity applies across the whole spiritual spectrum, which necessarily involves entire religions as much as it does individual persons or souls ... No matter how selfish our quest, it must involve every other creature in the universe, one way or another. Everything we do, and every thought we think has repercussions all around us for good or ill, whether we are aware of it or not. There is no such thing as a merely private morality or individual ethic – much less a private religion or spirituality. Once we try to cut ourselves off from others we have, to that extent, already diminished ourselves.'[148]

# 42

## We will know well when we're home

*Even now we are journeying towards ... our common home in heaven. Jesus says 'I make all things new' (Rev 21: 5). Eternal life will be a shared experience of awe in which each creature, resplendently transfigured, will take its rightful place ... knowing that all the good which exists here (this earthly home) will be taken up into the heavenly feast ... God has united himself definitively to our earth, and his love constantly impels us to find new ways forward. [LS 243, 245]*

Pope Francis prays that our struggles with ourselves and our planet may never take away the joy of our hope. He reminds us that in the heart of the world, in those times of disillusion and despair, 'the Lord of life, who loves us so much, is always present'. God is inextricably woven into the texture of our days and nights. Many believers desperately resist the notion of the ordinariness of our 'Everyday God', a God of the flesh, who comes to us disguised as our very own lives. But that is how we experience our divine Lover and Saviour in this life. Maybe it won't be all that different in heaven. If we are all so carefully fashioned in the image of our Creator-Mother, if humanity and all creation is the key to our understanding of heaven, then perhaps, instead of being a 'vale of tears' (as, indeed, it often is) this world is a kind of raw material to be transformed. This short poem by Emily Dickinson points out that heaven is not somewhere 'out there' in the future. It is here, now, within us, and surrounding us. Heaven is far more earthy than we suppose. If we fail to find it here, we won't recognise it anywhere else.

Who has not found the Heaven – below –
Will fail it above –

> For Angels rent the House next ours,
> Wherever we remove ...[149]

'All the good which exists here will be taken up into the heavenly feast ...'. Is Pope Francis persuading us about a new way of looking at Creation and all our experiences not as a preamble to heaven but as already the experience of it? 'Eternity has little to do with the hereafter,' wrote mythologist and Catholic writer Joseph Campbell. 'This is it. If you don't get it here you won't get it anywhere. The experience of eternity right here and right now is the function of life.' Maybe our future Resurrection will reveal that we have been experiencing it all our lives. We will have already felt it, 'proved on the pulse', as John Keats wanted. In *True Resurrection* Fr Harry Williams wrote, 'Heaven will be recognised as a country we have already entered, and in whose light and warmth we have already lived.'[150] According to these writers, then, we will definitely have a sense of déjà vu when we get to heaven!

There is a heresy called 'universalism' that Pope Francis seems to be flirting with in these extracts! One aspect of it is the belief that everything God has ever created will eventually be reconciled and saved for all eternity. Julian of Norwich was accused of this lovely (and apparently dangerous) opinion. Pope Francis puts this attractive belief as only he can: ' ... knowing that all the good which exists here (this earthly home entrusted to us) will be taken up into the heavenly feast ...'. It is really an effort to portray the holiness of the Earth, that nature too is heaven-bound. These words again remind us that if we never have glimpses and experiences of God's loving presence in the real presences of this life, then we will not recognise heaven after we die. All of this is not really surprising when we remember that God needed and desired to become our bodies, our senses, our emotions, our homes in time and space, so that divine being could be actually experienced everywhere, by everyone. It was with a view to experiencing an astonishing and redeeming intimacy with all of us that God created the world in the first place.

Poet Vladimir Holan wrote:

> Is it true that after this life of ours we shall one day be
> awakened
> by a terrifying clamour of trumpets?
> Forgive me God, but I console myself
> that the beginning and resurrection of all of us dead
> will simply be announced by the early crowing of the cock.
> After that we'll remain lying down for a while ...
> The first to get up
> will be mother ... . We'll hear her
> quietly laying the fire,
> quietly putting the kettle on the stove
> and cosily taking the teapot out of the cupboard.
> We'll be home once more.[151]

After all, if it was God's wish to become human through a mother who got up early to provide breakfast for her divine baby, why should we be surprised if that is how we meet God again? Yes, we'll know full well when we're truly home.

## A FURTHER WORD

*Pope Francis reminds us that God's love, incarnate in evolution, 'unites itself definitively to our earth, and constantly impels us to find new ways forward'. This compulsion is towards creating and completing, towards knowing and exploring; it is inherent in our very human nature, an essential part of our DNA itself.*

'It is part of our nature to love and to be honest. It is part of our nature to long to know more, and to continue to learn. Our knowledge of the world continues to grow. There are frontiers where we are learning, and our desire for knowledge burns. These frontiers of our learning are in the most minute reaches of the fabric of space, at the origins of the cosmos, in the nature of time, in the phenomenon of black holes, and in the workings of our thought processes. Here, on the edge of what we know, in contact with the ocean of the unknown, shines the mystery and the beauty of the world. And it is breath-taking.'[152]

There is a vision that allures and sustains us. Maintaining and nourishing that vision is a lifetime's work. Our whole life must be purified and intensified in the effort to become 'aligned' (St Paul) with the flow of the Holy Spirit in time and tune with the dance (perichoresis) of the Blessed Trinity in the core of our being, in the evolving heart of our planet. Is all of this new way of thinking what we once meant by 'the obedient doing of God's will', by 'humbly accepting what's in store for us'?

To be sure we honour our evergreen traditions. And most assuredly, too, there are new horizons coming into view. When Pope Francis suggests imagining heaven as carrying dimensions of our earthly home he is not just indulging in some pious or sentimental daydreaming. His suggestion is based on good theology. Planet Earth is not a place of exile to escape from; it is God's evolving body to be cherished and healed and transformed into a haven of peace for all Creation. Theologian Elizabeth Johnson gives us a glimpse of her dreams and hopes: 'A flourishing humanity on a thriving planet rich in species in an evolving universe, all together filled with the glory of God: such is the vision that must guide us at this critical time of Earth's distress, to practical and critical effect. Ignoring this view keeps people of faith and their churches locked into irrelevance with a terrible drama of life and death is being played out in the real world. By contrast, living the ecological vocation in the power of the Spirit sets us off on a great adventure of mind and heart, expanding the repertoire of our love.'[153]

# 43

## To be treasured and transformed

*He bears us on his shoulders ... With tenderness he restores our daily joy ...God loves us first, beyond each person's faults and failings ... the attraction of his love* (EG 3, 44)

Pope Francis holds that you cannot change the way God is in love with you, that his love flows all around you, and through you, and in you, and *as* you. You cannot lessen the divine love that is already and always, no matter what, wrapped tightly around your heart. You might as well try to separate the water from the wine. 'You cannot diminish God's love for you,' said Richard Rohr in one of his *Daily Meditations*. 'What you can do, however, is learn how to believe it, receive it, trust it, allow it, go with it, and celebrate it, accepting the Trinity's whirling invitation to join in the cosmic dance.'[154] He quotes a favourite line from Catherine LaCugna's book about the Trinity, *God for Us*; 'The very nature of God is to seek out the deepest possible communion and friendship with every last creature on this earth'. That is a way of naming God.

We do not need to become more loving to make God love us more. It is because God first loves us that we become loving in response. It is not because we pray more, become more religious and celebrate more sacraments that God looks at us with a greater love; nor is it because we go to confession that our sins are forgiven. Every single grace, every blessing of total love and forgiveness bestowed on us, no matter what efforts we make to earn it, deserve it, merit it, always and only spring from the unconditional divine love that created us in the first place. We have been loved from the beginning. Nobody was ever driven from a perfect garden. There was no primal 'original sin'; nor was it ever mentioned in the Christian scriptures. We seem to have missed out on the initial blessing that we are now, and always have been, and always will be.

But, misunderstanding the meaning of myth, the Church became preoccupied and trapped in the notion of a historic original sin, a preoccupation that has deeply damaged, to this day, the true meaning of the creation of humanity, the humanness of Jesus, the redeeming love of God and the divinity of our own hearts. Much of this book is about rebuilding, renewing and remembering our first foundation of original goodness, truth and beauty rather than on a basis of original disobedience, anger, sin and curse. 'We dug a pit so deep that most people and most spirituality could not get back out of it,' writes Richard Rohr.[155] We are carefully and wonderfully fashioned by a compassionate Mother-God who is captivated by us from our first breath, and is utterly devoted to us in our struggles and sufferings now, and who fills our spirit with the greatest longing for that final home-coming into the heart of the world, the heart of God.

Pope Francis writes a great deal about the attraction of this divine love that is the energy, health and well-being of our minds, hearts, souls and bodies. It is what keeps the world turning, the universe expanding. It is the breath of everything created, the beating heart of great and small. God's love attracts us to what is beautiful, what allures us to be beautiful ourselves, what keeps us believing in the dawn when our spirits are in darkness, what makes all Creation breathe his presence. The Pope is so anxious that we would consciously *experience* these sublime graces, that we would actually *feel*, with our senses, the pulse of being infinitely loved, continually reassured by that love, and always empowered to wrestle with the strange counter-attraction that haunts our hearts, that tempts us to fear, doubt, guilt and despair. For him, our experience of divine love is what matters more than all the catechisms, creeds and religious rubrics in the world.

We are all created for this purpose, to love and to be loved, to know and to be known. We grow by attraction; we are transformed by the experience of human and divine tenderness. 'Everyone longs for the comfort and attraction of God's saving love,' the Pope writes in *Evangelii Gaudium*, 'above and beyond their faults and failings'

(44). He refers to the attraction of all that is 'most beautiful, most free, most appealing. The *Message Bible* paraphrases St Paul in this conversational way: 'Summing it all up, friends, I'd say you'll do best by filling your minds, and meditating on things true, noble, authentic, compelling, gracious – the best, not the worst; the beautiful not the graceless; things to praise, not things to curse. Put into practice what you have learned from me, what you have heard and seen and realised. Do that, and God, who makes everything work together, will work you, too, into his most excellent harmonies.' (Phil 4:7-9)

The Pope longs for us to actually *feel* the gift of being utterly loved even in the midst of our winter of self-doubt; of being touched by the dawn while it is still midnight; of feeling comforted by the actual experience of our closeness to God. When describing the Eucharistic moment of receiving Holy Communion Pope St John Paul II speaks of 'a physical embrace'. At times we need more than words, he says. Our very human senses come into play even at this most sublimely divine moment. Notice Pope Francis's repeated use of fleshy words such as 'touched by', 'the comfort and attraction of God's saving love'. Only then will we *be* his saving presence for others. God *needs* us to keep incarnating divine love.

## A FURTHER WORD

> *Our deeper awareness of God's unconditional love transforms our own hearts with the divine energy. We strive to stay open to love; to embrace it; to become it as the Sunday bread and wine become us. It is the divine light of compassion that becomes enfleshed in our senses, and colours all we do and are.*

In *The Brothers Karamazov*, Fyodor Dostoevsky wrote: 'Love people even in their sin, for that is the semblance of Divine Love and is the highest love on earth. Love all of God's creation, the whole of it, and every grain of sand of it. Love every leaf, every ray of God's light.

Love the animals, love the plants, love everything. If you love everything you will perceive the divine mystery in things. Once you perceive it, you will begin to comprehend it better every day. And you will come at last to love the whole world with an all-embracing love.' For most of us it's the *awareness* that's missing. We cannot *attain* the presence of God because we're *already in* the presence of God. What we do not realise is that we are the very incarnation of God's love – a love that is maintaining us in existence with every breath we take. Every heartbeat means that God is choosing us now, and now, and now. The Buddha and Jesus are always whispering to us – 'Wake up. Stay watchful. You are living in the divine Presence. Be aware of who you already are – God's very own beauty in your human form.'

# 44

## The look of love

*'All people, no matter what, are God's handiwork, created in his image, reflecting something of divine glory, and the object of God's infinite tenderness, experienced in their lives.' 'We need to look at cities with a mystical gaze, a contemplative gaze of faith and imagination, seeing God dwelling in their homes, their streets and squares.' (EG 71, 264, 274)*

A friend, a grandmother and a mystic, sent me this observation. 'Small children have an astonishing capacity for wonder. With the simple act of turning to the next page of a picture book there's an excited cry, "Look! Look!" Each new image evokes delight, which is felt as keenly, perhaps even more so, as the book is read repeatedly and becomes a familiar friend. "Wow!" the little one exclaims with the same enthusiasm as he meets for the first time his new baby cousin. His eyes shine with unalloyed joy as he touches her tiny fingers, and his cries of delight bring smiles to those around him. There is total attention to, and engagement with each new moment. There is only *now*. The mystic in him is alive and thriving. It seems he can't help but look at the world with a "mystical gaze" and in his few words of excited response there is wonder and real pleasure. There is something beautiful in the moment as, intuitively and quite naturally, he seems to recognise the baby as the latest "handiwork of God". He has not yet lost the gift of seeing the world as God sees it, as God sees each one of us. His eyes are the eyes of God looking with infinite tenderness and love.'

Thankfully such moments are a graced but powerful reminder that all our encounters, our living of each new day, have the potential to awaken us to the presence of the divine flow of energy that permeates all that is. There is much letting go and unlearning to be done so as to see with the eyes of a two-year-old, but it is only through recovering that 'contemplative gaze', says Pope Francis, that we will look upon 'all people, no matter what' with tenderness and compassion. Only when we approach the places and people where we go about our daily lives, the streets and squares of our towns and cities, with the imagination and faith to see God dwelling there – only then will we begin to grasp more deeply the evergreen meaning of Incarnation, and become bearers of hope, healing and compassion for those who are limping along with their broken companions. Many people weep as they pray each morning for those facing another day of relentless brutality, torture and utter evil.

Pope Francis is calling us back to the essence of our Christian faith, that God's 'becoming human' in Jesus reveals and confirms the divine energy, the life force flowing through the universe, through all that is created and within each person. It is only in actual matter, in the physical form of the universe, in the humanity we all share, in the joys and anxieties of each person, in the everyday reality of our lives that we can encounter God. And it is only in those human encounters that we can experience acceptance and love, forgiveness and healing, courage and hope.

Pope Francis is calling for a radically different approach to evangelisation from the way we understood ourselves as determined missionaries in the past. He wants us to recognise, respect and affirm the holiness of each person as 'made in God's image and reflecting something of divine glory'. When we look at each person in the light of the Pope's incarnational words, we see, with that mystical gaze, that the tenderness called forth in us is the tenderness of God. It is easy to look at and delight in a newborn baby, to rejoice when we see snowdrops emerging as the first sign of new life after a harsh winter. Pope Francis, however, while waxing eloquent about these very realities throughout his *Laudato Si'* encyclical, is calling us to something much more profound, more radical and infinitely more challenging. He's asking us to look with infinite tenderness in all circumstances, wherever we find ourselves, and especially in the midst of our cities and their slums, far from nature, with poor people in poor places with little to admire.

When we encounter people living on the streets, or oppressed, burdened and marginalised, as the Pope did when ministering in Buenos Aires, with him we recognise that the only way their dignity can be restored is through our mutual interaction. The only way any of us can experience God's compassion and tenderness is through each other. That is the law of Incarnation. It is an astonishing realisation that we carry the power to heal and bless, to build up and restore, to co-create and sustain. But that is what the fleshing of God means. Surely then, the urgent task in our time is to recover the contemplative, the 'mystical gaze' that enables us to see God's intimate presence in every aspect of the daily round. (The 'Indwelling Blessed Trinity' is a very traditional expression.) This is what the incarnation of God disclosed, and what gives a Christian meaning to our journey through life.

And we have a reminder from the Pope that this vision and action takes much rethinking and much conscious effort. Through the practical example of his own ministry Pope Francis is trying to divest the Church of notions of power, prestige or privilege and recover instead the heart of the matter – a God of flesh whose only home is in the world around us, and whose only role is to build heaven here on Earth as we accompany and serve one another in tenderness and compassion. This graced habit, this blessed skill of acquiring a new way of seeing and being will one day become second nature to us.

## A FURTHER WORD

*The Pope writes of 'a contemplative gaze of faith and imagination'. This way of seeing reveals the same living core and energy of Being in all things personal, in all things universal. This sacramental vision also requires that we 'gaze from within', since we ourselves are in the heart of Creation, in the very heart of God.*

'As well as being the subjects who do the external observing of our environment ... we are also an integral part of the world we perceive. We are situated within it. Our view of it is from within its midst. We are made up of the same atoms and same light signals as are exchanged between pine trees in the mountains and stars in the galaxies ... We thought that we existed as unique beings, a race apart from the family of animals and plants, and discovered that we are descendants of the same parents as every living thing around us. We have ancestors in common with butterflies and larches ... Our moral values, our emotions, our loves, (our religions) are no less real for being part of nature, for being shared with the animal world, or for being determined by the evolution which our species has undergone over millions of years. Rather they are more valuable as a result of this: they are real. They are the complex reality of which we are made. Our reality is tears and laughter, gratitude and altruism, loyalty and betrayal, the past which haunts us, and serenity. Our reality is made up of our societies, of the emotions inspired by music, of the rich interwoven networks of the common knowledge we have constructed together.'[156]

It may help us to come to grips with the notion of universal 'oneness', the 'common being', that the Pope refers to, when we consider the amazingly close network of relationships that already exist, by virtue of Creation and evolution, between people the world over. Researchers have established that the vast majority of people in the world are linked by no more than two intermediaries. They have also concluded that two of the most isolated people on the planet – say a monk in Tibet and a hermit in Appalachia – are linked by no more than eight intermediaries.[157] Philosopher and scientist Guy Murchie wrote:

> What relation is a white man to a black man?
> A yellow man to a red or brown?
> Closer maybe than you'd think.
> For all family trees meet and merge
> Within fifty generations, more or less –

In round numbers a thousand years:
Which makes all people cousins,
Siblings in spirit if you will.
Or, to be genetically precise,
Within the range of fiftieth cousin.[158]

A theology of nature and grace as espoused by Pope Francis would bid us pursue the phenomenon of oneness still further. The fundamental interconnectedness and perennial allurement of all things for each other belongs to the exciting realms of deep Creation-centred mystery, and Incarnation-centred contemplation. As the physicists relentlessly explore the dark secrets of space, they confess to continual astonishment at the recurring patterns and harmonic flow that stem from, and tend towards a ubiquitous oneness. Having indicated this deep and mutual attraction, this intrinsic connection of all the families of Creation – human, animal, nature, space – Murchie continues:

There is no line, you see, between these cousin kingdoms,
No real boundary between you and the universe –
For all things are related ... [159]

# 45

## Seeing the face of God

*'Whenever we encounter another person in love, we learn
something new about God. Whenever our eyes are opened
to acknowledge the other, we grow in the knowledge of God,
opening up spiritual horizons, taking us beyond our limited
spiritual constructs.'* (EG 272)

Pope Francis is making a bold statement about the power of love and
the divine nature of every person. To learn something about God we
must experience human loving. And in loving another, the Pope says,
not only is a new window on God revealed, but our own horizons are
expanded, our hearts are stretched, and we reach beyond our limits.
There is a sublime scene near the end of the film *Les Misérables* that
captures something of what the Pope is claiming. After witnessing
the epic struggle of a people, the final message comes in the most
tender moment as Jean Valjean's life draws to a close. What endures
and what transforms everything is love, as the words of the song
proclaim:

> To love another person
> Is to see the face of God.

Such is the power of human love as portrayed in *Les Misérables*
that Archbishop Emeritus George Carey believes that some moments
in the film's story of the misery and ecstasy of human life contain
the finest description of grace outside the pages of the New Testament. St John Chrysostom wrote that 'Whatever unlocks the human
heart, unlocks the heart of God as well'. St Augustine said that the
love with which we love each other is the same love as that with
which God loves us. When costly, enduring love emerges between

people, something new and beautiful is created. Every healing that love brings to a lost soul is a sacramental event. In all the aspirations of the human spirit another face of God is revealed. This is incarnate spirit in time, place, flesh and free will. The mystery of faith, correctly understood, reveals that creation, evolution and all the capacities of humanity are revealed as embraced, healed and transformed from within by the God of Jesus.

For the Christian, any heart-wrenching story with its extremes of tragedy, ignominy and despair, with its searing emotion and passion, its human endurance in the face of utter loss and loneliness is, in faith and fact, the incarnate presence of the Christian God. There is no longer any competition between the world and God, between the secular and the sacred. The evolving planet Earth itself is, in fact, the body of God made visible. We no longer look up to the heavens for God; we now explore more deeply the human realities of our daily lives in an evolving world. Sacramental moments of intimacy with God are strewn all around us. These are the daily places of revelation. God materialises in human form – the only form in which God's love can ever be experienced.

But where is God, one might ask, in the terrible suffering, deception and cruelty at the core of our world today? Jesus spoke of the divine presence in the failures, the sinners, the criminals, even the evil ones of his time (Mt 25). So we believe that Jesus, in the fullness of his humanity, embraced and actually became the hopeless lives of the despised and condemned; that he experienced the utter degradation and humiliation of once beautiful bodies, the corruption and destruction of once brilliant minds. There are many unexplored and shocking revelations attached to that phrase we blithely and mindlessly repeat every time we say the Creed: 'He descended into hell'. Our wretchedly human God still looks out every evening from the televised hopeless faces of people ravaged by the mad greed and bloodlust of those who have forgotten their true nature and their 'true North'.

Yet where can the real presence and promise of the divine be physically and mentally experienced if not in the dark labyrinths of human hearts? And where else can there be the slightest evidence that God is an effective, invincible power healing humanity at its most desperate, most diabolic and most despairing, other than in the raw reality of our complicated, ambiguous and beautiful lives? Every day of his life, Pope Francis will be reminding us of this resisted revelation. *Les Misérables* (the wretched) carry a relentless belief in the breaking of 'the chains of slavery'. The exultant strains of 'the music of a people who are climbing to the light', who are singing of those 'chains [that] will never bind you' in that 'new world about to dawn', sounds like a kind of secular and graced Exultet, a redemption song of the people. 'To love another person is to see the face of God'. Dare we call it an elegant kind of mini-credo of the Christian faith?

## A FURTHER WORD

*'A big heart open to God'. Like an underground refrain running through all his writings, Pope Francis keeps reminding us of our 'magnanimity' – our potential for expansion, for abundance, our 'bigness', our innate capacity for self-transcendence, our constant searching beyond present boundaries. Notice his encouragement and support throughout* Evangelii Gaudium *for those trying to 'open spiritual horizons', 'to launch into the deep', 'to go beyond their limited spiritual constructs'. The Church is not a laboratory for certainties but a lover's vision of a God-permeated world. And, as we approach the end of this book, what is most important is that we ourselves, within our own hearts, must first become free and open in our personal spirituality and attitudes. The wildness of the Holy Spirit is invited in. The True Self must emerge. In his wee gem of a book,* The Calm Center, *Steve Taylor wrote:*

Don't make yourself a mask to meet the world
a mask that plays your life so well

that's so affable and entertaining
that you're always the centre of attention –
a mask you can't let slip, even for a second,
in case your real self shows through
and the audience realises that they've been
tricked and their affection turns to ridicule.

... Then your real self will stumble free
stunned after such a long imprisonment
dazzled by the brightness of the sun
reeling from life's complexity
naked and open to terror and delight.

And the world will trust you
the human race will welcome you
and slowly others will unmask themselves around you
as you feel yourself connecting to a deep
nourishing flow
beyond the fragile separateness of masks –
the richness of your being, opening to the richness
of others' beings, and of life itself
the wholeness of your being opening to the wholeness of life
        itself.[160]

# 46

## To become more truly human

*'The Son of God, by becoming flesh, summoned us to the revolu-
tion of tenderness ... making one more truly human.' 'Must be
incarnate – fleshy, with a face ... learning to find Jesus in the
faces of others, in their voices ... A mystical community capable
of seeing the sacred grandeur of God in every human being.'*
(EG 88, 91,92)

One of the most tender moments captured by the much loved and
greatly missed poet Seamus Heaney is his memory of being alone
with his mother when he was a child peeling potatoes for Sunday
lunch. The memory comes unbidden in all its fleshiness whilst he is
standing at her bedside with the rest of the family during her final,
precious hours. Suddenly Heaney has a vivid sense of his mother's
head bent towards his, their breaths mingling.

> So while the parish priest at her bedside
> Went hammer and tongs at the prayers for the dying
> And some were responding and some crying
> I remembered her head bent towards my head,
> Her breath in mine, our fluent dipping knives –
> Never closer the whole rest of our lives.[161]

Heaney touched so many people because of his capacity to see in
the most ordinary moments of human life the deep significance and
sacredness of what was happening. He may not use theological language, but so many of his poems capture powerfully how it is in the
everyday, human happenings and encounters that we experience love
and what Pope Francis calls 'the revolution of tenderness', that make
one 'more truly human'. When asked where he looks for holiness,

where he recognises God's presence, the Pope simply talked of a mother looking after her children or a father working hard to support his family. He is looking with the eyes of Incarnation, one who, like Heaney, can see into the depth of our humanness and recognise that God dwells there – not just in us, or through us, or all around us – but *as* us! To understand that shocking truth as much as possible is why we sit for a few minutes in contemplation each day; it is why we go to Mass on Sundays.

The Incarnation of God in humanity changes for ever our understanding of where we find 'sacred grandeur'. We look, not primarily to holy icons and paintings, or to churches and temples, but to people, to family, friends, colleagues and strangers we meet each day, to our humble comings and goings, to the vicissitudes of our lives. Whenever we see news clips of Pope Francis visiting a new country, or out and about in Rome, whenever we read reports of people who have met him, we see this profound belief borne out in his actions. He is constantly witnessing to a theology of Incarnation in the way he lovingly embraces vulnerable and wounded people, visits those in prison, reaches out to refugees with a natural tenderness and acceptance that raises up everyone he meets and makes them feel 'more truly human'. For Pope Francis, as for Jesus, the transformation of our world, the healing of pain and brokenness, the raising of people to their full dignity will happen only when we look at people with a 'contemplative gaze'.

When Iain was about eight years old, as a treat his mother took him into town to do some Christmas shopping. The station was crowded when they got off the train. Suddenly Iain's mother realised her son was no longer by her side and in panic she turned, only to see him standing, enchanted, in front of a poorly clad, unkempt man who was sitting on the ground begging. He was playing a mouth organ. As she retraced her steps she watched Iain bend down, speak to the man and put some of his pocket money into the upturned cap. Just as the mother was about to reprimand him for leaving her side, he stood and turned to her with a lovely light in his eyes and said, 'How lucky he is to be able to play such beautiful music.' Iain, quite naturally and without effort, saw only a graced and gifted human person and encountered him in love – a simple example of what Pope Francis means when he writes about seeing with the mind of Christ.

Blessed Oscar Romero's life was changed for ever when he opened himself to the experience of Salvadoran peasant communities. He wrote, 'It is entering into the reality of a child, of the poor, of those wearing rags, of the sick, of a hovel, of a shack. It is going to share with them. And from the very heart of misery, of this situation, to transcend it, to elevate it, to promote it, and to say to them, "You aren't useless. You aren't marginalized." It is to say exactly the opposite, "You are precious, valuable."'[162] It was not just that Romero had a one-off personal conversion, but he *recognised* that in the city slums, the very act of human loving itself brings about an inner transformation. He gave his life in love, knowing that such love will never be overcome but will always transform, and he lives on today, as he promised, in the Salvadoran people. Like Pope Francis, Blessed Oscar Romero learned to see the face of Jesus in the faces and voices of those who, while suffering themselves, reached out in love to others. He longed to create 'a mystical community capable of seeing the sacred grandeur of God in *every* human being'.

## A FURTHER WORD

*'A mystical community capable of seeing the grandeur in every human being.' Is there a recommended way of acquiring that sacramental vision into the deeper reality of all people and all created realities? Getting Creation and Incarnation 'right' is the key to understanding the wonder of* An Astonishing Secret. *Two prophets of our time, Sr Ilia Delio and Fr Diarmuid O'Murchu, open yet another window to help us grow in our efforts to deepen our grasp of the mystery.*

'To be related to the incarnation is to be related to one another and to all of creation. It means seeing the incarnation as the real presence of God in real time, in concrete material reality ... We tend to focus on the historical life of Jesus. He was a good man. He lived in Nazareth. He went about preaching the gospel, doing good things, healing the sick and raising the dead. We have this idea that if we dutifully follow the pattern of life Jesus laid down for us, we're guaranteed salvation.

'But to say Jesus is the Christ means that he is the long-awaited fullness of God's presence. What is the point of God taking on our humanity if it doesn't have meaning for us in our own humanity? The point is that just as Jesus is the Christ, we, too, are part of the Christ mystery, the Word-made-flesh, God's love incarnate, which has evolved through 14 billion years. As theologian Raimon Panikkar said, "Jesus is the Christ, but Christ is more than Jesus alone. Christ encompasses the whole cosmos".

'Incarnation is also about seeing the hiddenness of God. Francis of Assisi was very focused on the humility of God, who is hidden in everyday, ordinary reality. What do you see when you see another person? When you see a rabbit? A tree? A sand dune? Do you see only sand? Or do you see something more? We tend to treat the earth sort of like a backdrop for our lives. A "cosmic christology" reminds us that every aspect of the cosmos is in Christ, everything is Word incarnate. Everything bears the infinite love of God, each in its own way, which means that there's nothing earthly that doesn't have some divine dignity to it. God created the quark and the star, the bacteria, the snake. Everything reflects God in some way. Because every created thing has a relationship to God, I can't misuse, abuse, or control it. Cosmic Christology calls us to be in relationship to created things as a sister or brother. We are all part of the one cosmic family.'[163]

'Religious speculation on how God operates from afar, above and outside creation, has not served creation well and henceforth it is unlikely to provide us with an enlightened understanding of the divine at work in creation. The God of the evolutionary story is a life-force radically committed to creative, cosmic embodiment. God may be about many other things beyond this reality, but the major concern of evolutionary theology is that we take this dimension seriously. Contrary to previous times, it is not a case of understanding God first and then the world will make sense. Rather the world (created order) is God's first gift and revelation to us, and also the most enduring. It is precisely when we become enamoured with the elegance of the mystery at work in creation that we begin to discover a more enlightened way to apprehend the mystery and reality of God'.[164]

# 47

## Divine light of your human heart

*'Incarnation means that each human person has been taken up into the very heart of God, into a boundless love that ennobles each human being, conferring on them an infinite divinity ... We love this magnificent planet on which God has put us, and we love the human family which dwells there with its tragedies and aspirations.'* (EG 178)

As this book began, so it ends, with the meditative reflection of Rhineland mystic Mechtild of Magdeburg:

> The day of my spiritual awakening
>       was the day I saw and knew I saw
> all things in God and God in all things.[165]

Incarnation reveals that the energy pulsing within the universe, driving it ever onward and into eternity, is God's outpouring, creative love at the heart of the cosmos and in the heart of every person. Everyone is, therefore, a unique expression of that same dynamic of creative love that is always enabling and ennobling us to realise our enfleshed divinity, affirming that every aspect of our human experience is already sacred. It is the same force that spins the planets, shapes the baby, transforms pain, and brings us to our knees in adoration. And when we are caught up in that flow of loving energy, we know that love will always somehow prevail, 'even in the midst of tragedies that befall us'.

The implications of seeing through the lens of Incarnation in this way, 'of seeing God in all things and all things in God' are immense. They demand of us a *metanoia*, a radical conversion of heart and mind to a new way of seeing, a new way of being, and a revisioning of the role of the Christian community, the Church. It is Pope Francis's hope that, recognising the planet within which we live as God's body, and every person as a divine co-creator with God, we would take off our shoes and walk humbly and with reverence, cherishing our Mother Earth and each other. The everyday choices we make in terms of our use of natural resources, our patterns of consumption and our way of relating to one another, would be for the flourishing of our planet and of the whole human family. Compassion would be the leitmotif by which the Christian community would be recognised.

Faced with the divisions we see in our world, the poverty, violence and oppression of human families, together with the destruction and wanton depletion of Earth's resources, Pope Francis is making an urgent call for renewal at every level. He is wise enough to know, however, that first our own hearts must be set on fire with a vision that is compelling if we are to be innovators of this new reign of compassion. For the Pope, love is the touchstone, and he refers to Jesus loving 'this magnificent planet on which we are placed by God, and the people who live on it'. The starting point is to look anew with wonder and a great compassion at our earthly home. 'We are speaking of an attitude of the heart, one which approaches life with serene attentiveness, which accepts each moment as a gift from God to be lived to the full.'[166]

There is a powerful image that might serve to challenge us to recognise ever more deeply the power we carry. Can we begin to see ourselves as the latest, most complex expression of God's Creation? On the one hand we are Creation become self-consciousness through the divine flow of the evolving love within us now. And we are also, through Incarnation, the earthly embodiment of God. We could see ourselves then, first as a mirror, able to reflect back to Mother-Earth, in a way no other creature can, the beauty we behold, the beauty she is. And we could also truly think of ourselves as the fleshing of God's eyes through which God sees the world. There is much to contemplate in this way of perceiving our central, quite unbelievable role in the whole astonishing story of divine evolution – to be the eyes of both Creation and God. St Teresa tries to understand this mystery in the words the Risen Christ spoke to her about his need of her eyes, ears, tongue, if ever the world is to be saved. I offer another glimpse in a short meditation:

> And God said:
> May you delight in your body;
> it is my body too.
> Please see the world anew each day;
> how else can I behold my beauty?
> Fill the earth with the sounds of life;
> how else can I hear my song?
> May your skin rejoice in the passion of the sun;
> And your tongue tingle with the joy of new wine.
> Don't you know you are my senses? Without your
> body I cannot be here.

## A FURTHER WORD

*At this point you may be wondering if I'm really saying that we, sinful human beings, are, in fact already quite divine and, moreover, are happily on our way to becoming as God's own self. And I am. Let me explain. Unlike our Eastern Orthodox sisters and brothers, we in the west are somewhat unfamiliar with a most beautiful doctrine called 'theosis', or the deification and divinisation of humanity. Yet it is central to our whole lives, our birth and baptism, our belonging to the Catholic Christian community, our understanding of Creation and Incarnation. It lies at the core of the book you are now reading. Pope Francis expresses it so utterly delightfully and courageously: ' ... each human person has been taken up into the very heart of God ... conferring on them an infinite divinity*

...'. *St Athanasius of Alexandria summed it up when he wrote, 'God became human that we might become God.' St Bernard of Clairvaux asked, 'Why should we not become gods for Him who for love for us became man?' And the Catechism of the Catholic Church repeatedly affirms the Incarnational basis of this neglected teaching: '...man was destined to be fully human and fully divinised by God in glory...' (398); 'The word became flesh to make us partakers of the divine nature ... For the Son of God became human so that we might become God' (4601). We are all predestined by God for this astonishing transition, transformation and transfiguration. For that were we born and baptised. It is simply our salvation, our completion in full bloom, the natural culmination of life in Christ.*

'In his own inimitable style, C. S. Lewis in *Mere Christianity* puts it this way: '[God] said that we were 'gods', and He is going to make good his words. [That is] if we allow Him – for we can prevent Him if we choose. He will make the feeblest and filthiest of us into a god or a goddess, dazzling, radiant, immortal creature, pulsating all through with such energy and joy and wisdom and love as we cannot imagine, a bright stainless mirror which reflects back to God perfectly (though of course on a smaller scale) his own boundless power and delight and goodness. The process will be long, and, in parts, very painful: but that is what we are in for. Nothing less. He meant what he said.'[167]

# 48

## THE IRRESISTIBLE FORCE OF GRACE

*'Each day in our world, beauty is born anew; it rises, trans-*
*formed, through the storms of history. Human beings arise,*
*time after time, from situations that seemed doomed.' 'Where*
*all seems to be dead, signs of resurrection suddenly spring up.*
*It is an irresistible force.' (EG 276)*

This is not our usual way of talking about Easter! The Pope here is reminding us that the resurrection of the Human One, Jesus, serves only to point to a deeper reality named at the beginning of John's Gospel – that the Word, the eternal Logos, the Christ, is dying and rising at the heart of the cosmos every moment of every day from the beginning of time and into eternity, from the Alpha to the Omega of completed Incarnation. Woven into the fabric of the universe, scientists recognise, is the dynamic of dying to give birth to something new, and theologians are now beginning to recognise this process as the natural pattern of Christian Passover and Resurrection.

In what seems like death, destruction and darkness, life is already and always waiting to emerge, transformed into ever-new flowing forms and patterns of energy. There is, within the very essence of creation, cosmologists observe, from the original, spontaneous flaring forth of primal energy, a capacity to generate, die and re-emerge in ever more complex expressions of that same original energy. Within everything that exists, within each person there is, as Pope Francis says, 'an irresistible force', or 'love-energy', as Ilia Delio defines our experience of God within the universe, and within every human heart. We are invited to try to understand this as best we can, with the help of our friends, and our study and meditation.

'In the midst of darkness something breaks through,' the Pope continues. This 'something' is God's saving presence. The divine healing is always wrapped up deep in Creation, folded into the contours of nature, and into our own mysterious selves. 'God is in the life of each person' (*EG* 160, 44). Resurrection is always happening 'in the midst of darkness' – universally and personally. Grace is everywhere. It is always freely available to us. God's graciousness surrounds us on every side. It 'easters' the earth through its evolution; it urges us through the darker happenings of our days. Pope Benedict XIV emphasised the wider panorama of resurrection at a general audience in April 2011, when he spoke of it as 'the door to a new life that is no longer subjected to the termination of time, a life immersed in the eternity of God. With Jesus' resurrection begins a new condition of human being, which illuminates and transforms our daily path, and opens a qualitatively new and different future for all humanity ... Resurrection is the force that breaks down barriers and builds new harmony in love.'

Inspired by current scientific knowledge about the evolution of the universe, theologians offer a renewed and dynamic understanding of a universal resurrection. We struggle to understand this. They call us to a deeper realisation that all of Creation is 'groaning in one great act of giving birth' (Rom 8:22), that God is inherent in life itself, the life force of everything that emerges in Creation, and that the ultimate momentum is always and only towards greater growth and possibility. In this relentless movement, death is revealed not as the end, but as a transformative stage in the ongoing emergence of the universe, the painful journey towards harmony and unity.

The paradox of death generating new life is, then, the very essence of the observable universe, and it is at the very heart of our Christian faith. We see in the historic events of the passion, death and resurrection of the human person Jesus, the archetypal symbol of the Cosmic Christ signalling divine presence continually renewing the face of the earth. In *Quantum Theology* Diarmuid O'Murchu argues that our task as 21st-century Christians is to learn to befriend that paradox, and to trust the creative spirit within the miracle of our evolving universe. For it is this same spirit within which we 'live and move and have our being', and which will equip us 'with the wisdom to engage our world in a more enlightened, compassionate and justice-imbued way'.[168]

The problem is that we think we are still locked into a confining tomb of powerlessness when, in fact, the stone has been rolled away, calling us into a new consciousness, a new self-awareness, a new way of looking at the world and of seeing 'beauty born anew' each day. We are invited by Pope Francis to emerge into the light of a new reality where we see ourselves as part of the unfolding story of creation, already immersed in the infinity of which we have an inner intimation and a deep longing. The reality of the resurrection means, then, that each new day we can make the choice to live in the light, to enable the love energy of the universe to flow in and through us, and, for our children, to be co-creators of a future beyond our dreams.

## A FURTHER WORD

*The central doctrine of Christianity is, of course, the mystery of resurrection. Beyond the individual, one-off personal resurrection of Jesus at the first Easter there is, as we have just seen, an expanded and richer explanation of the continuing 'resurrection of all creation' in the light of an evolving universe. Resurrection names and reveals what is happening everywhere and all the time in evolution. Resurrection happens when death, even sin, all that normally destroys us, becomes part of what transforms and liberates us into a life bigger than all kinds of dying. Now we are indestructible. As Richard Rohr writes, 'All the tombs are empty: now there are no dead ends.' A panoramic view is opened up to us, a whole new blossoming is being affirmed; and the seeds of it were there from the very beginning. A priority for the Holy Spirit, at this particular time in the Church's history, is to astonish us with this revelation, Pope Francis's predecessor reassures us.*

Ilia Delio writes, 'If resurrection means new life, empowered by the Holy Spirit, a new future of embodied existence, how do we understand this new life in the context of evolution? In his 15th April 2006 Easter Vigil homily, Pope Benedict XVI described the resurrection of Jesus as "a qualitative leap in the history of evolution and of life in general towards a new future life". He said that the Resurrection was like an explosion of light, an explosion of love. It ushered in a new dimension of being, a new dimension of life in which, in a transformed way, matter too was integrated and through which a new world emerges ... It is, he repeated, a qualitative leap in the history of evolution toward a new world which, starting from Christ, already continuously permeates this world of ours, transforms it and draws it to itself ... The whole Creation is, in a sense, resurrection from the beginning. Evolution as God's creative act is the active self-transcendence toward new life.

'The resurrection recapitulates the whole evolutionary emergent creation as a forward movement to become something new, a new reign of God, a new heaven on earth. What took place in Jesus Christ is intended for the whole cosmos - union and transformation in the divine embrace of love ... Understanding the resurrection in a new, life-giving way is one of the most important tasks of theology today ... Earth is not left behind but transformed in love, and this transformation in love, here on earth, is heaven. What God promises is a new heaven and a new earth, not a new heaven without earth.'[169] 'Every act of physical death is an act of new life in the universe. The resurrection of Jesus speaks to us of this new life.'[170]

# 49

## PRIESTS AND PRIESTESSES OF THE HOME

*'What is holiness?' the Pope was asked. 'It is the mother bringing up her children, the father working to provide food for the family, those who suffer in silence, those who quietly serve others'.*
(EG 125, 129)

How would *you* answer that question? Would you talk to your questioner about being a Catholic Christian, avoiding sin, worshipping God, believing all the doctrines, observing all the rituals? Were you impressed by the Pope's reply? True to his fundamental and radical commitment to Incarnation, he instinctively recognised the core of holiness as basic family life, as creative love, as a healing, caring home and community. He knew that perhaps nowhere more than in the heartfelt dynamic of married life, where the human spirit stretches itself in its trusting and letting go to the limits of its potential, is this expression of incarnate love more clearly symbolised and sacramentalised. He helps us discover that every 'ordinary' human home is the unexpected place where God lives too. Even where there is suspicion and deceit, married life remains an epiphany of mystery, a participation in God's own challenging essence.

Any time we say to each other 'I'm trying to love you, to forgive you', or 'I still believe in you, trust you', that is also the ever-present expression of God's incarnate covenant with us, and within us, constantly healing and completing each day, all that is imperfect. As we know by now, there are no longer two kinds of love, of forgiveness – a divine level and a human one. Incarnation has revealed and confirmed that every genuine human emotion is ratified in heaven. Everything human and everything divine have now become one. Our very lives are God's only and preferred way of completing us, saving and divinising us, intimately and always loving us.

And all of this is happening in the living rooms and kitchens of every family. The home is, indeed, a holy place. It is the nursery of divinity. It is the really real church. As midwives of mystery, the work of most parents is unrelenting. Their whole lives are spent in coaxing and persuading, with the 'mother-tongue' (a beloved phrase of Pope Francis), from within reluctant shadows into the light of day, God's fleshed, unfamiliar beauty. It is the continuing of Incarnation, the fleshing of real love. The role of the institutional church, with its doctrines and sacraments, is basically to 'mother' that holy place, to protect it, heal it, nourish it, purify it and intensify it.

And there is an urgent energy within our domestic world waiting to be released into the church. The home is a cauldron of emotions, all now charged with redemptive presence; for that reason it is also a powerhouse of renewal within the church. The passions and prayers, the storms and whispers, the blame and the blessing – are all part of that graced energy. Everything that happens in the unbelievably complex fabric of family life, the light and dark of it, has God's life-giving heartbeat within it, God's loving signature set to it. And we go to Mass on Sundays to remember that; to celebrate together the extraordinary revelation that no moment in family life or outside it is 'merely' human or worldly or secular, but rather a place of grace. Every threshold, 'every gate', as St Catherine of Siena put it, 'is a gate to heaven'.

Marriage and family is the gate, the threshold through which couples go in hope to reach their fullest potential. Partners save or destroy each other to the extent that they draw out the true self, the *imago Dei*, in each other – or not. And what is surprising is that this comes about, not because of marvellous promises or achievements, but in the most ordinary events, attitudes, relationships and duties of the home. It is so often a great comfort and consolation for parents to see the daily demands of their married life in the light of Incarnation, where everything is revealed to be potentially 'full of grace'. Catholics go to Mass to be assured of this.

'I have come to realise', reflected a mother at one of our sessions before the second Synod on the Family (2015), 'that everything that serves the life of our home is holy – the daily baths, the messy meals, responding to calls for a drink of water in the middle of the night, the laundry, the bills, the hurting, the forgiving'. It is as though God has invested the most common and menial acts of loving duty with extraordinary, transformative powers. The greatest places of intensity of human love are the places of the profoundest divine presence. In the early Christian community parents were called 'the priests of the domestic church', consecrating the daily bread, the nightly tears, the constant sacrifice – these informal, raw and messy sacraments of the home. 'Holiness in the family takes on a very ordinary appearance.'

It needs to be urgently added that marriage and family life is also a kind of symbol or climax of the hidden holy attraction begun in Creation that makes evolution and Incarnation possible, that drives the long and loving universe story to the end of time when God will be 'all in all'. From the first 'flaring forth' of the Big Bang there is a fundamental attraction at the heart of Creation and evolution. That love-energy of God is the essential core in the becoming of all life, at all levels of development. It is marvellously personalised and symbolised in human love, marriage and family. In *Models of God*, theologian Sally McFague opens for us another window of wonder: 'There is a passion in the universe; the young stars, the whirling galaxies – the living, pulsing earth thrives in the passionate embrace of life itself. Our love for one another is the language of a passionate God ... It is desire that spins us around, desire that sends the blood through our veins, desire that draws us into the each other's arms, and onward in the lifelong search for God's face. And in the love of one another we see that face – in the touch of each other's hands we feel God's presence.'[171]

## A FURTHER WORD

*A final reminder. One of the truths that burns at the heart of evolution, insofar as we understand the phenomenon, is our kinship with Creation, with nature, with stars and planets, with the almost 14 billion years of our infancy. All those realities are, in fact, emerging from the very womb of God, carrying the seed of God. 'Just as the pear seed becomes the pear tree,' wrote Meister Eckhart, 'and the maple seed becomes the maple tree, so too, God's seed in us blossoms into God'. In some way, then, that we most certainly do not understand, the expanding cosmos, the travail of nature, the 'groaning' Earth are healed a little, reconciled and celebrated, when a human couple get married.*

Creation had waited for billions of years to achieve self-consciousness (in us). Once this breakthrough was accomplished, the cosmos then needed to celebrate its incredible life story with its mysterious beginning, its hazardous evolution, its split-second timing and its relentless love-energy. For with the advent of humanity – its new, first and unique heart and mind – this became possible. And the sacrament of marriage is one of its rich expressions.

### The Setting

Let the music of the spheres be our wedding song
and the wonders of the world our bouquet.
Let Mother Earth be our altar
and Sister Sky our cathedral canopy.
We are honoured to have the trees, the mountains,
the seas and the animals, the fish and the birds
as the witnesses of our marriage at this holy and timeless
    hour;
to have the dawn chorus as our Sanctus.
We are the loving mind of the universe;
we are the human heart-focus of eternal love,
and when we become one this moment
the evolving cosmos dances for a second time.

## *The Invocation*

In the name of North and South,
of East and West;
in the name of Earth and Wind,
of Fire and Water;
in the name of Summer and Winter,
Spring and Fall;
in the name of the first Fireball and the last Sun;
and in the name of the Love
we call God ...
our human and cosmic hearts and bodies
complete, in each other, the erotic impulse of Creation.

## *The Exchange of Vows*

I vow to set you free to be your truest self –
by the power of our love.
I vow to bestow upon you, the gift of your deepest being –
by the power of our love.
I vow to reveal to you the wonder of your beauty –
by the power of our love.
And may the holy heart of the universe bless and complete us
this moment;
may its holy energy grace our every breath and heart-beat;
and, beyond our wildest dreams, may our human love
bring to birth a fragile and eternal beauty.[172]

# ACKNOWLEDGMENTS

This book is dedicated to the brave and curious theologian and scientist in the heart and mind of you, the reader. In spite of relentless distractions, the desire to keep searching for the truth about our deepest, beautiful spirit, and about the love-story of our evolving universe, keeps growing. May we do all we can to honour the stories of Creation and Incarnation, to nourish them in our graced imagination, eventually to actually incarnate in our own flesh something of the unfolding fire and mystery of God. And then to allow others to catch the light from us – even as we radiate with their light too. That is how the world and the Churches will one day be saved.

I thank Margaret Siberry, Martin and Maria Bennett, Andrew and Marita Thompson; also Garry O'Sullivan, Michael Brennan and Alba Esteban of Columba Press, Fiona Biggs and all the people over the years with whom I have shared something of the living heart of the evolving mystery of love.

# NOTES

1.  Opening Prayer for the 17th Sunday in Ordinary Time/Year A. Old Translation. *The Roman Missal.*
2.  Richard Rohr, *Daily Meditations,* 2 March 2017: https://cac.org/inner-outer-worlds-converge-2017-03-02/
3.  Tom Inglis, *Meanings of Life in Contemporary Ireland.* New York, NY: Palgrave Macmillan, 2016, p. 139.
4.  Thomas Berry, *The Dream of the Earth.* San Francisco, CA: Sierra Club Books, 1990, p. 123.
5.  https://w2.vatican.va/content/john-paul-ii/en/letters/1988/documents/hf 19880601 padre-coyne.html
6.  Greeting of his Holiness Pope Francis to participants at the conference organised by the Vatican Observatory, 12 May 2017.
7.  Sue Woodruff, *Meditations with Mechtild of Magdeburg.* Rochester, VT: Bear & Co., 1982, p. 46.
8.  Denis Edwards, 'Resurrection and the costs of evolution: A dialogue with Rahner on noninterventionist theology', in *Theological Studies* 67, 2006. http://cdn.theologicalstudies.net/67/67.4/67.4.4.pdf
9.  Ilia Delio, *The Emergent Christ.* New York, NY: Orbis Books, 2011, pp. 153, 156.
10. Ibid., p. 110.
11. Ibid.
12. Kevin Treston, *Who do you say I am?* Melbourne: Morning Star Publishing, 2016, p. 7.
13. Ilia Delio (ed.), *From Teilhard to Omega: Co-creating an Unfinished Universe.* New York, NY: Orbis Books, 2014, p. 13.
14. Kevin Treston, *Who do you say I am?* op. cit., p.120.
15. Karl Rahner, 'Natural Science and Reasonable Faith', in *Theological Investigations.* New York, NY: Crossroad, 1988, p. 48.

16. Thomas F. O'Meara, *Vast Universe*. Collegeville, MN: Liturgical Press, 2012, p. 99.

17. Alexander Carmichael, *Carmina Gadelica*. Berwick-upon-Tweed: Lindisfarne Press, 1992, p188; quoted in GLAS, Trócaire, Ireland, p. 47.

18. Jacintas Shailer SGS, *Wildflower Journey Prayers*. Rainbow Books, 2007; quoted in GLAS, Trócaire, Ireland, p. 11.

19. Quoted in GLAS, Trócaire, Ireland, p. 10.

20. Ilia Delio, *The Emergent Christ*, op. cit., pp. 114, 115, 117.

21. Karl Rahner, *Foundations of Christian Faith: An Introduction to the Idea of Christianity*. New York, NY: Seabury Press, 1978, p. 111.

22. Judy Cannato, *Fields of Compassion: How the New Cosmology is Transforming Spiritual Life*. Notre Dame, IN: Sorin Books, an imprint of Ave Maria Press, 2010, p. 71.

23. Ilia Delio, *The Emergent Christ,* op. cit., pp. 57, 58.

24. Matthew Fox, *Original Blessing*. Sante Fe, NM: Bear and Company Inc., 1983, p. 119.

25. Hugh O'Donnell, *Eucharist and the Living Earth*. Dublin: Columba Press, revised edition, 2012.

26. Zachary Hayes OFM, *A Window to the Divine*. Winona, MN: St Mary's Press, 2009, pp. 75, 76.

27. Ilia Delio, *The Emergent Christ*, op. cit., p. 57.

28. Ilia Delio, ibid., p. 46.

29. Ilia Delio, ibid., pp. 50, 55.

30. Gerard Manley Hopkins, 'God's Grandeur', in *Gerard Manley Hopkins: Poems and Prose*, London: Penguin Classics, 1985.

31. Elizabeth Johnson, *The Quest for the Living God: Mapping Frontiers in the Theology of God*. New York, NY: Continuum, 2007, p. 189.

32. Ilia Delio, *The Emergent Christ*, op. cit., p. 103.

33. Pierre Teilhard de Chardin, *Science and Christ*. London and New York, NY: Collins and Harper & Row, 1968, pp. 34–36.

34. Ilia Delio, *The Emergent Christ*, op. cit., p. 113.

35. Ursula King, *Pierre Teilhard de Chardin*. New York, NY: Orbis Books, 2012, pp. 27, 29.

36. Brian Swimme, *The Universe is a Green Dragon*. Sante Fe, NM: Bear and Company, 1984, p. 162.

37. R. S. Thomas, *Collected Poems 1945–1990*. London: Orion, Phoenix Giants, 1993, p. 221.

38. Richard Rohr, *Morning Meditations*, 31 July 2017: http://cac.org/you-are-the-image-dei-2016-07-31/

39. William G. Joseph, unpublished paper, 2016.

40. Jack Mahoney SJ, *Christianity in Evolution*. Washington, DC: Georgetown University Press, 2011.

41. Pierre Teilhard de Chardin, *Christianity and Evolution*. Quoted in William G. Joseph, *But what is a Soul?* CreateSpace Independent Publishing Platform, 2016, p. 219.

42. Ilia Delio, *The Emergent Christ*, op. cit., pp. 33, 45.

43. Herbert McCabe, *Faith Within Reason*, ed. Brian Davies. London: Continuum, 2007; reproduced in *The Tablet* as 'Self-confessed sinners', 5 March 2011.

44. Ursula King, *Pierre Teilhard de Chardin*, op. cit., p. 124.

45. Pope St John Paul II, General Audience, 17 January 2001.

46. Richard Rohr, *Daily Meditations*, 19 November 2016. cac@cacradicalgrace.org

47. In Maria Shrady, *The Cherubinic Wanderer* (Classics of Western Spirituality). Mahwah, NJ: Paulist Press, 1986, p. 37.

48. Ilia Delio, *The Emergent Christ*, op. cit. p. 58.

49. Ibid. pp. 91, 79.

50. Pope Francis, Address to the United Nations General Assembly, New York, 25 September 2015.

51. Wendell Berry; quoted in *Spiritual Ecology: The Cry of the Earth*; Llewellyn Vaughan-Lee (ed.). London: Golden Sufi Centre, 2013, p. 77.

52. Pierre Teilhard de Chardin, *On Love and Happiness*. London and New York: Collins and Harper Brace, 1984.

53. Ilia Delio, OSF, *Christianity in Evolution*. New York, NY: Orbis

Books, 2008, pp. 18–19.

54. Brian Swimme, *The Universe is a Green Dragon*, op. cit., p. 40.

55. Ibid., p.19.

56. James Finley, *Jesus and Buddha: Paths to Awakening*. Albuquerque, NM: Center for Action and Contemplation: 2008, disc 2 (CD, DVD, MP3 download).

57. Brian Swimme, *The Universe is a Green Dragon*, op. cit., pp. 52, 57.

58. See *Gaudium et Spes*, Documents of Vatican II, 36.

59. Elizabeth Johnson, *Ask the Beasts: Darwin and the God of Love*. London: Bloomsbury, 2014, p. 150.

60. Ibid., loc. cit.

61. Pierre Teilhard de Chardin, *The Phenomenon of Man*. London and New York, NY: Collins and Harper & Row, 1959, p. 312.

62. Joseph P. Provenzano and Richard W. Kropf, *Logical Faith: Introducing a Scientific view of Spirituality and Religion*. iUniverse, Inc. 2007, pp. 34, 36, 37.

63. Ilia Delio, *The Emergent Christ*, op. cit., pp. 107, 108.

64. Pierre Teilhard de Chardin, 'The Spiritual Energy of Suffering' in *Activation of Energy*. London: Collins, 1970, pp. 247–48.

65. Pierre Teilhard de Chardin, 'The Significance and Positive Value of Suffering', in *Human Energy*. London and New York, NY: Collins and Harper & Row, 1969, pp. 48, 51–2.

66. Plenary Session of the Pontifical Academy of Sciences, Casina Pio, 27 October 2014.

67. Elizabeth Johnson, *The Quest for the Living God: Mapping Frontiers in the Theology of God*, op. cit., p. 191.

68. Dylan Thomas, 'Fern Hill' (1945), in *Deaths and Entrances*. New York, NY: New Directions Corp., 1952.

69. John O'Donohue, *Walking on the Pastures of Wonder* (in conversation with John Quinn). Dublin: Veritas Publications, 2015, pp. 58, 59, 61.

70. Richard Rohr, *Daily Meditation*, 16 November 2016.

71. Elizabeth Johnson, *The Quest for the Living God: Mapping*

*Frontiers in the Theology of God*, op. cit., p. 198.

72. Christoph Quark (ed.), *Mysticism for Modern Times: Conversations with Willigis Jäger*. Liguori, MO: 2006. Quoted in John Feehan, 'Reflections on the presence of God in creation', private paper, 2016, p. 23.

73. Paul Ricoeur, *Philosophie de la Volenté, t. 2: Finitude et Culpabilité*. Paris: Seuil, 1960, 2009 edition, p. 216.

74. Carlo Carretto, *Love is for Living*. London: Darton, Longman & Todd, 1976, p. 19.

75. Sam Keen, *The Passionate Life*. New York, NY: Harper & Row, 1983, p. 192.

76. Dylan Thomas, 'The Force that Through the Green Fuse Drives the Flower', in *The New Penguin Book of English Verse*. London: Penguin, 2000, p. 909.

77. Brian Swimme, *The Universe is a Green Dragon: A Cosmic Creation Story*, op. cit., pp. 94, 95, 162,

78. Thomas Aquinas, *Summa Theologica*; 1, 47, i.

79. Brian Swimme, *The Universe is a Green Dragon: A Cosmic Creation Story*, op. cit., pp. 18, 28, 39, 40.

80. Ibid. pp. 59, 60, 61.

81. Karl Rahner, *The Eternal Year*. London: Burns & Oates, 1964, p. 91.

82. Ursula King, *Pierre Teilhard de Chardin*, op. cit.

83. Diarmuid O'Murchu, *In the Beginning was the Spirit*. New York, NY: Orbis Books, 2012, pp. 82, 83.

84. Pierre Teilhard de Chardin, *Writings in Time of War*. London and New York, NY: Collins and Harper & Row, 1968, pp. 60, 64.

85. Diarmuid O'Murchu, *In the Beginning was the Spirit*, op. cit., p. 169.

86. Ibid., pp. 203, 204 [18].

87. John Donne, 'No Man is an Island'.

88. Fritjof Capra, *The Unification of Physics* http://www.fritjofcapra.net/the-unification-of-physics/

89. Ursula King, *Pierre Teilhard de Chardin*, op. cit., pp. 55, 57.

90. Judy Cannato, *Field of Compassion: How the New Cosmology is Transforming Spiritual Life*, op. cit., pp. 60, 77, 149–150.

91. John Macmurray, *Freedom in the Modern World*. London: Faber & Faber, 1932, p. 218.

92. Richard Harries, *Art and the Beauty of God*. London: Mowbray, 1993, p.145.

93. Zachary Hayes OFM, *A Window to the Divine*, op. cit., p.78.

94. See *Gaudium et Spes*, Documents of Vatican II, 22.

95. Richard McBrien, *Catholicism*. London: Chapman 1984, p. 1042.

96. John F. Haught, *Mystery and Promise: A Theology of Revelation*. Collegeville, MN: The Liturgical Press, 1993, p. 163.

97. Pierre Teilhard de Chardin, *Le Milieu Divin: An Essay in the Interior Life*, op. cit. pp. 34, 37.

98. 'Lord purge our eyes to see', in *The Complete Poems of Christina Rosetti*, Vol 2, ed. R. W. Crump. Baton Rouge, LA: Louisiana State University Press, 1986, p. 210.

99. Noel Dermot O'Donoghue, *The Mountain behind the Mountain,*. Edinburgh: T & T Clark, 1993, p. 61.

100. Kathleen Raine, 'The Wilderness', in *Collected Poems*. London: HarperCollins, 1981, p. 107.

101. Ursula King, *Pierre Teilhard de Chardin*, op. cit., pp. 82, 84.

102. Bill Plotkin, *Nature and the Human Soul: Cultivating Wholeness and Community in a Fragmented World*. Novato, CA: New World Library, 2008, p. 7.

103. Joanna Macy and Molly Young Brown, *Coming Back to Life: Practices to Reconnect our Lives, our World*. Gabriola Island, BC: New Society Publishers, 1998, p. 21.

104. Judy Cannato, *Field of Compassion: How the New Cosmology is Transforming Spiritual Life*, op. cit., p. 35.

105. Diarmuid O'Murchu. *Evolutionary Faith*. New York, NY: Orbis Books, 2002, pp.623, 73, 93, 122, 206.

106. Edward O. Wilson, *The Future of Life*. London: Little, Brown, 2002, p. 151.

107. Eckhart Tolle, *The Power of Now: A Guide to Spiritual*

*Enlightenment.* London: Hodder & Stoughton, 2001, p. 79.

108. Daniel O'Leary, 'The Litter Picker', unpublished poem.

109. Zachary Hayes, OFM, *The Gift of Being: A Theology of Creation.* Collegeville, MN: The Liturgical Press, 2001, p. 123.

110. Ilia Delio (ed.), *From Teilhard to Omega: Co-creating an Unfinished Universe,* op. cit., pp. 12, 13, 19.

111. Hugh O'Donell, Eucharist and the Living Earth. Dublin: Columba Press, 2012.

112. E. F. Schumacher, *This I Believe.* Cambrige: A Resurgence Book, an imprint of Green Books Ltd, 1998, p. 30.

113. Ursula King, *Pierre Teilhard de Chardin,* op. cit., pp. 14, 23, 24.

114. Pierre Teilhard de Chardin, 'Cosmic Life', in *Writings in Time of War.* Glasgow: William Collins and Sons & Co., 1968, pp. 60–2, 64–5.

115. Desmond Tutu, Ubuntu Women Institute USA, uwi-usa. blogspot.be/2012/01/Ubuntu-brief-meaning-of-africa-world. html

116. Karl Rahner, *Foundations of Christian Faith: An Introduction to the Idea of Christianity.* New York, NY: Crossroad, 1985, p.195.

117. Judy Cannato, *Fields of Compassion: How the New Cosmology is Transforming Spiritual Life,* op. cit., p. 54.

118. Quoted in Daniel O'Leary, *Windows of Wonder.* Dublin: Columba Press, 1991, p. 153.

119. Joseph Campbell with Bill Moyers, *The Power of Myth.* New York, NY: Doubleday, 1988, p. 22.

120. Elizabeth Johnson, *Ask the Beasts: Darwin and the God of Love,* op. cit., pp. 13, 14.

121. Nicholson and Lee (eds), *The Oxford Book of English Mystical Verse,* 1917.

122. Brian Swimme, *The Universe is a Green Dragon: A Cosmic Creation Story,* op. cit., p. 19.

123. Teilhard de Chardin, *Le Milieu Divin: An Essay on the Interior Life.* London and New York, NY: Collins and Harper & Row, 1960, pp. 13–16, 108–9.

124. *The Complete Mystical Works of Meister Eckhart*, Maurice O'Connell-Walshe (ed.), revised by Bernard McGinn. New York, NY: Crossroad, 2009, p. 275.

125. Adapted from James Findley, *Christian Meditation: Experiencing the Presence of God.* San Francisco, CA: Harper San Francisco, 2004.

126. Pierre Teilhard de Chardin, *Writings in Time of War*, op. cit., pp. 69–70.

127. Judy Cannato, *Field of Compassion: How the New Cosmology is Transforming Spiritual Life*, op. cit., p. 59.

128. Denise Levertov, *Breathing the Water.* New York, NY: New Directions Books, 1984.

129. Ursula King, *Pierre Teilhard de Chardin*, op. cit., pp. 120, 121, 122.

130. Michael Skelley, *The Liturgy of the World: Karl Rahner's Theology of Worship,* A Pueblo Book; Collegeville, MN: The Liturgical Press, 1991, p. 100.

131. Pierre Teilhard de Chardin, *Le Milieu Divin*, op. cit., pp. 126, 128–130.

132. John Macquarrie, *Principles of Christian Theology.* London: SCM Press, 1966, p. 398.

133. Gregory Baum, *Man Becoming*, New York, NY: Herder and Herder, 1970, pp. 75, 76.

134. Thaddeus Guzie, 'Theological Challenges', in *A Symposium on Christian Initiation*, W.Reedy (ed.). New York, NY: William Sadlier Press, 1979, pp. 168, 169.

135. Pierre Teilhard de Chardin, 'The Christic' in *Heart of Matter.* London and New York, NY: Collins and Harcourt Brace Jovanovich, 1978, pp. 93–6.

136. Pierre Teilhard de Chardin, 'The Mass on the World' in *Heart of Matter*, op. cit., pp.130–34.

137. Pope St John Paul II, *Theology of the Body.* London: Pauline Press, 2006, 55.2.

138. Ben Okri, *Birds of Heaven.* London: Phoenix Books, 1996, p. 9.

139. R. S. Thomas, *Collected Poems 1945–1990*, op. cit., p. 166.

140. Pierre Teilhard de Chardin, 'The Mystical Milieu' in *Writings in Time of War*, op. cit., pp. 144–7.

141. Pierre Teilhard de Chardin, *Hymn of the Universe*. London and New York, NY: Collins and Harper & Row, 1965, pp. 19–21.

142. Pierre Teilhard de Chardin, *Le Milieu Divin: An Essay on the Interior Life*, op. cit., pp. 116–18.

143. Quoted in Elizabeth Johnson, *Truly Our Sister: A Theology of Mary in the Communion of Saints*. New York, NY: Continuum International Publications Inc, 2003, p. 165.

144. Judy Cannato, *Fields of Compassion: How the New Cosmology is Transforming Spiritual Life*, op. cit., p. 47.

145. Ilia Delio, *The Unbearable Wholeness of Being: God, Evolution and the Power of Love*. New York, NY: Orbis Books, 2013, pp. 179–180.

146. Brian Swimme, *The Earth is a Green Dragon*, op. cit.

147. Dylan Thomas, 'The force that through the green fuse drives the flower', op. cit., loc. cit.

148. Joseph. P. Provenzano and Richard W. Kropf, *Logical Faith: Introducing a Scientific View of Spirituality and Religion*. iUniverse, Inc., 2007, pp. 83, 84.

149. Emily Dickinson, 'Who has not found the heaven – below', in Ivan M. Granger, *The Longing in Between*. Poetry Chaikhana, 2014, p. 60.

150. Harry Williams, *True Resurrection*. London: Mitchell Beazley, London, 1972, p. 13.

151. Vladimir Holan, 'Resurrection', in *Narrative Poems 1*. Bury St Edmunds: Arima Publishing, 2008.

152. Carlo Rovelli, *Seven Brief Lessons on Physics*. London: Penguin Books, 2014, pp. 78, 79.

153. Elizabeth Johnson, *Ask the Beasts: Darwin and the God of Love*, op. cit., p. 286.

154. Richard Rohr *Daily Meditations*, 30 September 2016: https://cac.org/god-is-for-us-2016-09-30/

155. Richard Rohr, *Morning Meditations*, 8 July, 2015: http://cac.org/original-blessing-2015-07-08/

156. Carlo Rovelli, *Seven Brief Lessons on Physics*, op. cit., pp. 64, 73, 74.

157. 'The Shrinking World', in *Bottom Line Research*, Vol. 10, No. 3, February 1989.

158. Guy Murchie, *The Seven Mysteries of Life*. New York, NY: Houghton, Mifflin & Harcourt 1999, p. 649.

159. Ibid. p. 701.

160. Steve Taylor, *The Calm Center: Meditation for Spiritual Awakening,* selected by Eckhart Tolle. Novato, CA: New World Library, 2015, p. 28.

161. Seamus Heaney, 'Clearances 3', *New Selected Poems 1966–1987*, London: Faber & Faber, 2013, p. 227.

162. Oscar Romero, *Through the Year with Oscar Romero,* trans. Irene B. Hodgson. London: Darton, Longman & Todd Ltd., 2006, p. 117.

163. Interview with Sr Ilia Delio, in *U.S. Catholic* magazine, April 2011, Vol. 76, No. 4, pp. 19–20.

164. Diarmuid O'Murchu, *Evolutionary Faith,* op. cit., p. 129.

165. Sue Woodruff, *Meditations with Mechtild of Magdeburg,* op. cit.

166. Ilia Delio, interview with Christopher Lamb in *The Tablet*, June 2014.

167. C. S. Lewis, *Mere Christianity.* London: Macmillan, 1984, pp. 174, 175.

168. Diarmuid O'Murchu, *Quantum Theology: Spiritual Implications of the New Physics.* New York, NY: Orbis Books, 2004, p. 105.

169. Ilia Delio, *The Emergent Christ,* op. cit. pp. 75, 76, 77, 98.

170. Ilia Delio *The Francis Factor: How St Francis and Pope Francis are changing the world.* CAC MP4 video.

171. Sally McFague, *Models of God.* Minneapolis, MN: Fortress Press, 1987, p. 130.

172. Daniel O'Leary, *Year of the Heart.* Mahwah, NJ: Paulist Press, 1989, pp. 158–61.